Conversations

Second Edition
Updated & Expanded

How to Survive an Active Shooter

What You do Before, During and After an Attack Could Save Your Life

Jacquelyn Lynn

Conversations

How to Survive an Active Shooter

What You do Before, During and After an Attack
Could Save Your Life

2nd Edition

Jacquelyn Lynn

Copyright © 2018 by Jacquelyn Lynn

All rights reserved. No part of this publication may be reproduced, distributed or transmitted in any form or by any means, without prior written permission.

Please employ this book as an aid to understanding general trends in active shooter type engagements. Readers are encouraged to build upon this information and prepare their own approaches to their future safety. Incidents mentioned which have significance to any similar situation should be researched thoroughly to understand the full scope of information applicable to each individual and personal environment.

This publication is designed to provide accurate and authoritative information regarding the subject matter covered. It is sold with the understanding that the publisher and author are not engaged in rendering legal, accounting or other professional services. If legal advice or other expert assistance is required, the services of a competent professional person should be sought.

Cover Design: Jerry D. Clement
Production: Tuscawilla Creative Services, LLC

Tuscawilla Creative Services, LLC
P. O. Box 1501
Goldenrod, FL 32733-1501

www.CreateTeachInspire.com

How to Survive an Active Shooter: What You do Before, During and After an Attack Could Save Your Life / Jacquelyn Lynn – 2nd ed

ISBN: 978-1-941826-23-2

In honor of the many
precious souls who dedicate
their lives and careers to
keeping us safe.

CONTENTS

Introduction to the Second Edition 1
Introduction 3
What is an Active Shooter Situation? 5
What Should You Do When the Unthinkable Happens? 11
How Does a Shooter Prepare? 17
What Should You Do When the Shooting Starts? 29
When Do You Call 911? 67
What Do You Do When Law Enforcement Arrives? 71
What Should You Do When You Get Outside? 73
How Should You Respond to Questions from the Shooter?. 75
How Do Multiple Shooters Operate? 79
What Weapons are the Attackers Using? 83
How Do You Handle a Hostage Situation When You're the Hostage? 97
Does the Motive of the Shooter Matter? 101
Do You Have Additional Tips for Safety in Public Places? 107
What Specific Advice do you have for Protecting Houses of Worship from an Attack? 111
Can You Teach Children to Survive an Active Shooter Situation? 133
Final Thoughts 139
About the Expert 145
Appendix 151

Introduction to the Second Edition

A lot has happened since the first edition of *How to Survive an Active Shooter* was published. The names of more places that were once known to us simply as towns and cities where people live, work and visit are now synonymous with a mass killing event. The perpetrators have added new tactics along with weapons other than firearms to their arsenals. Innocent people are feeling vulnerable in places we once felt safe.

If you're feeling frightened, helpless, and hopeless, stop! Even as we see these horrible attacks occur, we see amazing courage, and that alone should give us hope. If we are prepared to face an attack, we are not helpless and that should also reduce our fears.

The goal of this second edition, as was the goal of the original, is to provide knowledge and tools to keep you and your loved ones safe should an attack occur. We updated and expanded the original content but have still kept this as a book you can read in a couple of hours—an investment of time that could save your life and the lives of those you hold dear.

Jacquelyn Lynn

Introduction

On June 12, 2016, I was going through my usual Sunday morning routine and saw a news alert that there had been a shooting at a downtown Orlando nightclub. I thought it must have been some sort of drunken spat that escalated, and I continued getting ready for church. On the drive to church, I heard on the radio that an estimated 20 people had been killed in that shooting. As I tried to begin processing what that meant, I didn't realize they hadn't finished counting the bodies. By the time I was leaving church, the number of dead was up to 50 (49 victims plus the shooter).

Suddenly my hometown, known as one of the most popular tourist destinations in the world, had a new distinction: home to the worst mass killing by an active shooter in the United States.

A few weeks later, a member of our church offered to give a presentation for the community on issues related to the aftermath of the massacre. His career has focused on anti-terrorism issues with military and law enforcement, so he was able to talk about Islamic extremist terrorism, the methods and ideologies behind the attacks, and what we can expect in the future in terms preparing for future attacks. He also talked about what to do if you find yourself in an active shooter situation and what can be done to turn victims into survivors.

I thought that information was so important, so valuable that I asked if he'd sit down with me for a Conversations book on the topic. He agreed, with the caveat that I couldn't use his name because of the nature of his work.

This book is an edited version of our interview presented in a Q&A format.

An editorial note: We refer to a single shooter with masculine pronouns (he, him, his) for simplicity's sake. While there have been some female mass murderers, such as one of the San Bernardino shooters, the overwhelming majority of mass murderers have been male.

When you've finished this book, please share it with someone you care about. It could save their life.

Jacquelyn Lynn

CHAPTER ONE

What is an Active Shooter Situation?

Question: *Let's begin by defining an "active shooter situation."*

Answer: What's interesting is that a lot of the official definitions are changing to fit the current reality. My belief is that you stick to basic English. In an active shooter situation, you have someone with a firearm who is actively attempting to kill others in mass numbers. To me, that is an active shooter situation.

However, when you start to deal with a lot of the larger scale threats that are targeting the American people in general, including those coming from abroad, and the Islamic extremism faction, we often are dealing with an explosive charge being involved as well as firearms. Some other tactics may be applied in addition to that, so the term is gradually migrating to include guns and explosives.

Q. *So, from a broad, overview perspective, what are the types of threats or events that we are seeing now or might see in the future?*

A. We have seen an evolution of the tactics perpetrators are using. Many of the threats previously seen only overseas are now on American soil, and more may migrate here over time. We may need new definitions of phrases like "active shooter situation" and other terms we have become familiar with. Those intent on advancing their deadly "craft" will continually learn from their predecessors and find new ways to kill in higher numbers. At present, guns, bombs, and automobiles have all been used as means of mass killing in the United States. If you look overseas, you will also see lethal gas, the emergence of drones, and combinations of bombs and vehicles, guns and bombs, or other lethal pairings. Sadly, as those who seek to do harm learn to be more effective, we will see the more proven methods move to the United States. Other tactics will also emerge.

In the meantime, also notice what has *not* come here. Think about terrorism-based hostage situations, the attempted use of sarin gas in the Tokyo subway, the series of attacks perpetrated (and attempted) in Barcelona, and other events you have seen overseas.

If an attack was effective and the perpetrators escaped, you can expect to see that method of attack repeated more frequently. If the attack was minimally lethal, or the perpetrators were rapidly brought to justice, then that method will be either shelved or "improved" upon until it becomes effective.

The landscape and methods of terrorism and killing will keep changing. If you pay attention to what derives the most terror, the most media attention, and the most carnage, that will be the next wave that you see come to our shores in the USA.

But for the purpose of this book, I would still say to stick the raw definition of the firearm with the intent to kill multiple parties as our central theme.

Q: Active shooter situations—with and without explosives—are becoming so much more frequent than they used to be. At least, it seems that way. We know that the media plays into this and the 24/7 news cycle makes us aware of events we might not have noticed in the past. But is that perception accurate and, if it is, why is it happening?

A: I have looked up statistics on that very question. The Voice of America put out a news bulletin that covers this issue, and this is what it said:

In July 1984, we had a gunman who killed 21 people at a McDonald's in California.

In 1986, we had a gunman kill 14 postal workers in Oklahoma before he committed suicide.

Then we had two incidents in 1991 at the University of Iowa and at a Texas cafe.

In 1999, we had the Columbine incident that killed 12 students, a teacher, and the two gunmen.

In January 2006, seven years later, we had an ex-postal worker who killed eight before committing suicide in California.

In October 2006, a gunman killed five girls in a Pennsylvania Amish school and committed suicide.

In April 2007, a Virginia Tech student killed 32 people before committing suicide.

Then in November 2009, an Army psychiatrist killed 13 people at Ft. Hood, Texas.

Now, that's a good-sized list, but from January 2011 through June 2016, we have had a total of nine additional active shooter events across the country with six in 2015 alone. And of course, we had the one here in Orlando that occurred in June 2016 leaving 49 dead. Then a bombing in May 2017 at an Ariana Grande concert in England killed 22. In October 2017, a shooter in Las Vegas killed 59 people when he fired down into a crowd from a high-rise hotel. All of those incidents demonstrate a change in tactics taken since the shooting at the Pulse nightclub in Orlando, and these new attacks may have been informed by the lessons learned from the high casualty rate of the Pulse shooting.

So, yes, the statistics are there to back up the assessment that active shooter situations are becoming more abundant.

As far as what is causing them, there are a lot of theories. What I will share is my personal belief that we have a nation right now that has ceased to focus on where we are unified and begun to instead focus on where we are divided. And it takes that division and uses it to sell media stories. Those stories become sensationalized, the situations become overstated, they become over-amplified.

It's also important to point out that the media only cover the events that include death and destruction. The events that are thwarted are not spectacular enough to warrant placing into our consciousness.

We also have a society that no longer deals with fact and official documentation. We have a society that deals with social media-based emotion and opinion, and we spend more time in frenzies over emotion than I have ever seen in my lifetime.

Take that now and realize that you have that microcosm working to cause stress on the citizens of this country, then realize that it broadcasts abroad. And abroad, when you look at the terrorist cells that are attempting to work against the American interest, they now are seeing not only the ability to demonize America in the eyes of their followers but to say, "Look at what the Americans say about themselves, they deserve this." We are in many ways, through the shifts in our culture, inviting this growth in ways we have not even begun to understand.

CHAPTER TWO

What Should You Do When the Unthinkable Happens?

Question: Let's talk about why it's so important to know what to do if you find yourself in an active shooter situation. Certainly, it's good to understand the cultural and political issues that are causing the increase in these incidents, but the primary goal of this book is to teach people how to survive if they find themselves in an unthinkable situation with someone trying to kill them—and as many others as possible. I would think part of the answer to the question of why it's important to know what to do is because the chances of it happening to you were once so remote, and now they're not so remote.

Answer: That's a fair statement. Generally, you have two primary motives for an active shooter.

You have a person who is upset with a situation in a given environment, such as an employer or workplace—the old phrase "going postal" resulted from a lot of postal workers being removed from their jobs. Management gave nothing but negative feedback, attempting to motivate them to leave their jobs. Instead many of them reacted by simply cracking and coming in and killing their co-workers and bosses. That reality still exists in today's economy and today's stressors.

The other thing you have is somebody who has demonized everyone of a given category. These are the people who come to a site and decide which people to kill, such as everyone of a certain religion or race. And then you will have situations like the Pulse nightclub in Orlando, where you have somebody who had geared himself up with such a hatred for Americans—and I use that term intentionally, I do not believe that the LGBT community was specifically targeted. He wanted to kill Americans; he believed that was his imperative as someone who believed the teachings of Islamic extremist terrorism. That being the case, everyone in that place was his enemy. He wanted to kill as many as he could.

The students at Columbine—it was the same situation. They wanted to kill as many as they could. The man in the Colorado movie theater, the same thing. They had created a demonization of the people and had to kill them.

If you are on the other end, there is no talking your way out of this, there is no reasoning your way out of this. You are facing a person who does not know you, yet hates you with every fiber of his being. How do you deal with that? There are tactics that we will go into on how to handle that situation, but the most important thing you need to understand is that it is a situation you can face and there is no reasoning a way out of it.

Q. That was the same situation with the guy who killed nine people in a church in South Carolina.

A. Whenever you have a gunman who is coming in and attempting to kill mass numbers of people, especially those he does not even know, you are in this mentality: "Someone has done wrong to me and I am building up to hate them, and when I hate them I will destroy them." That is the mentality they are coming with. You will not become their friend; you will not reason with them. They have come to that conclusion and have come to execute that plan.

Q. So the reality is, once you're in this situation, you're not going to be able to talk the perpetrator out of it. You need to accept that, right? What are the keys to being prepared for such a situation before the attack, the shooting, actually begins?

A. There are a couple of things in our society that we don't really consider as being an issue in surviving an active shooter situation.

The first one is how to react when you see odd behavior. You would typically avert your gaze, you will look away, you will diminish yourself, you will hide from it. The challenge is that you now empower the evil actor by doing so. You are giving him strength by doing that.

The best thing to do is when you see that odd behavior, let him know you are on to him. Make him think that you know what's in that head of his. Let him believe that someone has found him out. That is the first key to your safety. Be alert and show that you are alert.

Think about the stereotypical movie-based elderly woman with her purse who gets mugged on a street. She's diminished, she's hiding herself, she's crouched down, she's clutching that bag with fear, she's looking away from the assailant. The assailant can creep up on her, sneak up behind her, take advantage of her, pick that purse or injure her.

What happens if you reverse the situation? When the would-be assailant sees her, she looks him dead in the eye, and she walks away with a confident stride and posture? What gets changed in the mind of that assailant? "Oh, she can identify me." "Oh, she knows what I'm up to." He really wants another target. Unfortunately, we've been trained to look away and hide—to allow that targeting to occur. I'm sorry, that's not the answer to your question.

Q. *It's still good information. But we're not talking about a street mugger.*

A. Anytime you have an active shooter, if they have prepared for the event, they have chosen their target. The Pulse nightclub in Orlando, if you ever look at a diagram of it, was a place with no escape route. Everything led to a fenced-in wall and blocked-in area, and the place had been cased by Omar Mateen, the shooter. He knew that the doors had been barred shut, that the one door was not functioning. He came in through the only exit that could have allowed people to retreat. He was shooting fish in a barrel, and he planned that.

Think about the movie theater in Colorado. The shooter researched and found that that particular theater would offer him no opposition, as it was a gun-free zone. He chose it because of that. He wanted the fish-in-a-barrel situation. No one could really get out very well; they were trapped.

So what's your best answer to be prepared? If you go into a place where you are with a group of people that could be targeted, know your exits, know your path out, know how you are going to leave if you need to. If you can determine multiple paths to exit the situation, then identify at least three of them.

Your first rule will be to flee. We'll get into this more later, but of course you are not going to flee if while you are in that room and it's being attacked, your child is in the bathroom and about to come back, or you're on one side of the building, the people you love are on the other.

You're going to have some decisions to make. But you need to know where those exits are, no matter what you decide to do. We'll go into more about what your options are later. Just remember that if you don't know where the exits are, you're not likely to be able to get out.

Q. That's an excellent point. I hadn't thought about addressing the issue of what to do if, as a situation unfolds, you are separated from people you care about, and you don't want to abandon them.

A. You'll have some hard decisions to make, and you'll have to make them in a flash.

CHAPTER THREE

How Does a Shooter Prepare?

Question: What leads up to the actual active shooter situation? I understand there's the psychological side, the radicalization and so on, but from a more practical, nuts-and-bolts perspective, how does the shooter prepare for the attack?

Answer: We're talking about two different types of shooters.

One is somebody who has been disaffected and angered by a situation. He wants to deal with that situation in a very vengeful, angry way. He wants to target and kill specific people. He may not care who else is in the way.

With the other type of shooter, you also have the radicalization factor. The radicalization factor is saying that "it is your duty to kill, it is your responsibility to kill, and this is your path to salvation, that you must kill."

These are different motives, but what is common is both types of shooters will have to go through a process that changes them, that changes how they look at people, how they look at that environment. It changes how they appear in it each day.

I still wonder in the Mateen situation [Orlando Pulse nightclub shooter]—he had gone to Pulse long before he shot it up. I wonder how much they saw him change and how many people shied away from him and didn't look at him as this was occurring. He was allowed to morph right in front of them, and they turned their backs because that is how our culture normally handles this. We need the reverse in order to be safe.

Similarly, in the workplace, if somebody is becoming very enraged, their personality will shift, and as that shift occurs he will become more and more angry, he will become more and more verbal, there will be more and more desperate statements that are kind of scary, and there needs to be a mechanism by which these changes can be reported.

Going through these visible changes is part of the ways they prepare. They also will go and pick up their weapons—their firearms, their explosives, whatever other devices they plan to use. They may use locks, they may use 2x4s—whatever they need to create the environment they need to achieve their goal.

And now I'm going to share with you something that hasn't usually been brought into this dialogue of understanding how shooters prepare for their attacks. If you want to see something amazing, take a look at the way the Israelis protect Tel Aviv Ben Gurion Airport, probably the most difficult airport to secure on the planet. They regularly tell the Americans that we're approaching it all wrong. We as Americans have a habit of looking for devices. We do it in our airports; we do it for active shooters. We think about the gun, we think about the bomb, we think about the knife.

Ben Gurion Airport doesn't do that. At Ben Gurion Airport, when you come in to take a flight, you're interviewed. There are people who will pick up certain aspects about the people about to board those aircraft. They will notice tendencies in the people, and then from those tendencies pick up on who are people of interest.

At Ben Gurion Airport they go after the person. At La Guardia, they go after the device. Ben Gurion has never had a hijacking.

When you start to think about that, you start to realize, if a person wishes to kill they will get a weapon suitable to their desires into a situation.

If you go back to 9/11, there was no bomb, and there was no gun. The box cutters that ultimately brought down the planes didn't come on board with the attackers. They got them onto the plane through other means and then leveraged them. You don't need to bring a weapon on board with you to be lethal. So, as you take a look at that and talk about how the shooter prepares: He changes his mindset, and then we chase after a device. Once again, we are going backward.

We need to pay attention to the people. Don't turn our backs, look them in the eye, pay attention, listen to them, see them, report them, and catch them.

Q. But most people reading this are likely to be thinking that they don't want to confront someone they think might be dangerous.

A. Nor do they need to.

If it's a person in the workplace, most likely you're dealing with a person you know. They come in angry because the boss gave them a bad performance review. The next day, they're saying, "I'm gonna kick his butt." Then the next day, it's, "I'm so fed up with him I'm gonna take a 2x4 to his head." You will see an escalation.

The means should exist within the workplace to report that escalation and deal with it, to get that person to counseling, to get that person assistance before the event unfolds. If the person is ignored, it will grow and fester.

In the case of the radicalized individual, this may happen in private. Now, I'm using the Pulse example because it's so recent and so local to us here, but if you take a look at that, Mateen had to have gone through a process to be ready to kill all those people.

He was casing the place to determine how to do it effectively. He was changing. There were people in his presence. Had they noticed him, they had some opportunities. One is, by him being noticed, he would have thought twice about carrying out his plan. He would have thought somebody might know what he was doing. The other challenge is that, had they seen him, someone may also have offered him some sort of consolation or assistance and may have changed his path completely before he had committed to the act of a mass killing. That's not confrontation. Confrontation may be necessary when the person is actively engaged in the attack. All the predecessor times and periods give other opportunities to dissuade them, to assist them, to redirect them in a non-confrontational way.

Q. But Dylann Roof, the young man who killed all those people at that church in South Carolina—they welcomed him into their church, they prayed with him, and he killed them anyway.

A. And why did he go into the church?

Q. In the beginning—

A. Did he go in to pray or to kill? He was already there. I mean, mentally and emotionally he was already in the mode to kill.

Q. I see. What you're saying is that once someone gets to that point where he's walking in with his weapons and his plan, there's no negotiating. Any intervention would have to come far sooner.

A. Correct.

Q. Okay, we've talked about how the shooter prepares and some of the behaviors that might be visible in the weeks or maybe even months leading up to the attack—the changes in personality as the attacker becomes committed to his plan. What happens in those moments right before the attack? Is there a way to know that you need to flee before the bullets start flying?

A. You mean when the moment of the attack is imminent, when we're right at that hairy edge when it's about to occur?

Q. Yes.

A. Let's look at what you have. You have a person who is built up with determination to commit the deed, to kill the people.

You're sitting in church, and they walk in. You're sitting in the mall, and they walk by. You're in school, or work, or a restaurant or wherever. They're not going to be a normal person walking by, and you may even sense it. There will be hairs standing up on the back of a lot of necks because people will sense that something is about to happen. Something is wrong with this person—they stand out from the crowd. Their anger, their rage, their purposeful movement tell you that something is amiss.

Now, I've told you to look them in the eye, let them know you've seen them, use your own awareness to make them rethink their plan. But if that doesn't dissuade them and they walk on by, and if you're at that point in their progression, that's what is going happen—they're going to walk right on by you because they don't want to deal with you right now. And as they walk by you, you know that this is somebody you don't want to be around. So go. Leave. Get away.

Now if, for example, your child is in the bathroom so you can't just leave, maybe you want to get right on that person's heels and follow him, and grab the next club you find. Maybe you want to make sure, when your child comes back into that area that is now a danger zone, that you are ready to respond the moment that person pulls out his weapon.

Q. But he hasn't done anything yet. What happens if he just happens to be eccentric?

A. Then you are never going to take action, but you will be ready. You will be in range, and you will be ready.

Now, this is the challenge of the situation. There is no single answer. It may be you alone. If it's you alone, leave. But it may be you and 20 of your closest friends. It may be you and your dearest family members. It may be you and your mother in a wheelchair. It may be you and your child in the bathroom.

Each situation is going to change what you think is the right action. So if your desire is to get away and you can get away, do so. Put as much distance between you and them as you can, and that will save your life.

On the other hand, if you have to engage them, be ready to do so. And if you do, understand that the moment you commit to that action, you will do it every ounce of your being because what you will be opposing is every ounce of theirs. There is no halfway here.

Q. So you are saying you need to really trust your intuition in these situations, am I right? Because thinking about the articles in the news reports that I've read about all these situations, people did seem to have a sense that it was getting ready to happen.

A. Yes.

Q. But they even though they sensed it, they often did nothing.

A. Correct, because that's what we are taught. We need to unteach that. We need to unlearn that.

Q. Okay, our intuition is likely to be on target.

A. Correct, but within reason. You are not going to attack someone because you feel something is awry. You are instead going to prepare to engage against this person. You may grab something to hit them with, but until they are a proven threat, you will not hit them with that item. You are preparing here—not acting on the impulse. If something is wrong, you are *preparing* to address it, not ignoring it. You are therefore ready for the worst case but have not violated any laws nor caused any harm. If you ignore the situation completely, then you are only preparing to be a victim.

But remember, every situation will be different. If you've been standing in line for three hours at the DMV and there are only two people ahead of you, you may decide to stay close to him, let those hairs stick up on the back of your neck and just pay a lot of attention to that person—and you should. And the moment things start to go south, get out. If you can.

Q. What are some of the things a shooter considers when choosing a target? I understand that if it's a workplace issue, that's where they're going to go. But for the shooter that just wants to kill as many people as possible, what are they looking for?

A. Remember that I talked earlier about the issue of shooters choosing sites where nothing they did was opposed. Almost every single active shooter incident has been in a gun-free zone. They chose their targets because they knew they wouldn't have opposition.

There have been exceptions. I mentioned the attack in Texas in 1991, where a man drove a pickup truck into Luby's Cafeteria in Killeen, got out and started shooting. He killed 23 and wounded 27 before he killed himself. That was not a gun-free zone. But by driving the pickup truck through the wall, plowing over a whole bunch of people, and then engaging in shooting, he negated their ability to react to him.

This is part of the process of their preparation. They want to kill as many as possible. That means they want to live as long as possible. However, I believe it's only two percent of shooters get out alive. And, by the way, 50 percent are taken down by unarmed civilians, because that's the targets they choose—places with unarmed civilians. Armed civilians take down 25 percent of shooters, and the rest are taken down by police.

To show just how significant they plan for non-interference, look at failed attempts. Attempts at schools in Pearl, Michigan (10/1/97), Parker Middle School (4/24/98), the Appalachian School of Law (1/16/02), the New Life Church (12/9/07) are a few among many other examples where attackers failed to achieve mass casualties. The death toll in Columbine was reduced the same way—by opposition.

Because someone fought back—many with firearms on site—many survived the incidents. Of particular note is the Clackamas Town Center Mall incident in Oregon (12/11/12), where a shopper ignored the gun free zone markings and showed a firearm to the assailant. In response, the assailant committed suicide.

What is amazing is the size of this list of thwarted attacks missing from our media. The shooters are often fragile people not ready for opposition. School shootings that have been thwarted over the past decade number far more than the total of *all* mass shootings that have been successful on a large scale.

In the United States, these occurred in Green Bay, Wisconsin on 9/14/06; Plymouth Meeting, Pennsylvania on 10/11/07; Mishawka, Indiana on 6/4/08; Pottstown, Pennsylvania on 9/4/08; Drexel Hill, Pennsylvania on

3/11/09; Monroe, New York on 10/21/09; Tampa Bay, Florida on 8/17/11; Albany, Oregon on 5/27/13; Seattle, Washington on 7/3/13; Cumming, Georgia in 9/13; Trinidad, Colorado on 12/20/13; Danbury, Connecticut on 3/4/14; Waseca, Minnesota on 5/1/14; and Plain City, Utah on 12/1/14—all school shooting attempts that were successfully thwarted. This is the part of the killer psyche we don't hear about in the media. We only see the ones where there were mass killings.

We remember the big ones—the six dead in Lancaster County, Pennsylvania (10/2/06), the 33 dead at Virginia Tech (4/16/07), the six dead at the Northern Illinois University (2/14/08), the seven dead at Oikos University in Oakland, California (4/2/12), the 28 dead at Sandy Hook Elementary in Newtown, Connecticut (12/14/12), the six dead in Santa Monica (6/7/13), the five dead at Marysville, Washington (10/24/14), the ten dead in Roseburg, Oregon (10/1/15), and the six dead police in Dallas near El Centro College (7/6/16).

If many of those sounded unfamiliar to you, then realize that someone in government or media decides what the term "mass" means in "mass shooting" each time. I listed the ones with five or more dead as mass shootings, yet for the most part that is not enough to enter our media nor our long-term memory. Why not?

We also need to realize where we stand historically. The first school shooting took place in 1764. There were 224 school shootings recorded in the 20th century. As of July 2016, we already have 178 school shootings in the 21st century. The year 2014 alone saw 35 such incidents. If this trend continues, we will see 1,079 school shootings in this century—a 606 percent increase. Something is happening to our people to generate all this hatred. As I said at the beginning, our people are focusing on their differences—not their similarities—and they are blaming devices for the deeds of people. Our culture has changed, and we are suffering for it.

Incidentally, there have also been a dozen school *bombings* in the 20th and 21st centuries. Domestically, these appear to be on the decrease, but several are combined with shooting attacks. While terrorists are increasing their use of bombs overseas, our schools have already faced domestic terrorism involving explosives. The 1970s concentration often involved protest bombings, carried out with either a racial integration or anti-war sentiment; and the Unabomber is a unique situation. However, where did the justification come for the five bombings of the past 30 years?

For the record, those school bombings were: Bath School, Bath Township, Michigan (1927); Poe Elementary School, Houston, Texas (1959); University of Wisconsin-Madison, Wisconsin (1970); Ayden-Griffin High School, Pitt County, North Carolina (1971); Kanawha County, West Virginia (1974); Olean High School, Olean, New York (1974); Unabomber attacks (including two at Northwestern University, IL; two at University of California-Berkeley; one at Yale University; and one at University of Michigan-Ann Arbor, 1978-1995); Cokeville Elementary, Cokeville, Wyoming (1986); Cleveland Elementary, Stockton, California (1989); Columbine High School, Columbine, Colorado (1999); University of Oklahoma, Oklahoma (2005); Hillsdale High School, San Mateo, California (2009).

Since this list was compiled, there have been many more incidents. The FBI is publicly stating that the growth in active shooter situations is evident. While I don't believe it's necessary to continually update a list that keeps getting more frightening, what is important to note is that the methods of mass killing are evolving. So long as the motivations remain, there will be those seeking to improve or perfect their skills at killing. In the last year, the most significant events have been the bombing at the Ariana Grande concert in Manchester, England, the mass shooting in Las Vegas, and the targeting of pedestrians by killers armed only with their vehicles. These are not all active shooter incidents but are clearly acts along that continuum motivated by the same factors to achieve the same end result: mass casualties and media/social media attention.

CHAPTER FOUR

What Should You Do When the Shooting Starts?

Question: When the shooting starts, when the slashing begins, whatever the weapon of choice, what are the basic tactics for survival? Let's start with an overview then go back and talk about each one in more detail.

Answer: Let's start with what you *shouldn't* do or what people do wrong. I'm not blaming the victims by any means, but what you shouldn't do is as important as what you should do.

If you look at the Pulse nightclub shooting: You have a man walk in with weaponry to kill a lot of people, and they were packed one on top of another for him to shoot at. As he fired that weapon and as he ran out of ammunition in the magazines and put in new magazines, not a soul opposed him. They couldn't get out, but they didn't bring him down.

They lit their faces up in dark rooms with cell phones to stay in touch with others and tell them what was going on. They left buzzers and ringers on. There's a problem with that tactic.

Now let's go to Virginia Tech. The students sat at their desks and in walked the gunman. He began to shoot them in the side of the head, and he walked from desk to desk to desk, and they sat silently and let him do it. One classroom after another. And no one opposed him. The weapons he was carrying were such low-caliber that very little would have been needed to shield them from his shots. Nobody got up from their desk. They sat and let him kill them.

In Columbine, the shooters came in, they included propane bombs in their attack methodology, and as they walked through and began to shoot, the teachers followed the training they were given. They stopped the students from fleeing the building and told them instead to hide under tables and desks and stay in place. Many of them died because of that decision. In fact, reports verified by 911 tapes say that Eric Harris, one of the Columbine shooters, poked his shotgun under a table where students were hiding, said, "Peekaboo," and killed a student hiding there.

These are the tactics that are being employed today, and they don't work. So now, when you are saying what does work, again, there are a million answers.

Of the classes I've taken, the books I've read, the best approach I've seen is the WIN or "What's Important Now?" principle.

Ask that question at every moment: What is important for me right now? WIN: What's important now?

The reason you do that is that is to determine if you are worried about the child coming from the bathroom, the mother in the wheelchair, the 30 friends on the other side of the building, or your own life. You will identify what is important at that moment and you will then know what you need to do.

Do you wish to save your life? Worry about their futures and fates? Do you wish to stay and help make their lives continue? That's a judgment call that will be on every individual in every situation to make.

Once they know what's important, they need to commit to that decision and act it out. They can rethink it every five seconds, but they need to commit to it enough to take that action. So maybe they need to hide, wait until the situation is in a different scenario, the shooter is at a greater distance, something like that, and then they can scoop up that child, that wheelchair-bound person, the friends, and get out. Maybe that's their choice.

Maybe their choice is to run and hope for the best and say a lot of prayers. Maybe their choice is that they want to find the first weapon they can and oppose that individual doing the deed. Those are the choices that they have to make, and it's going to be an individual decision based on each individual situation. Did I answer the question?

Q. Not completely. If I understand you, you're saying that you need to quickly decide what tactic you're going to use and do it. The basic tactics are to run away; if you can't run away, then defend yourself; and if that doesn't work, oppose and defeat—meaning oppose the shooter and defeat the weapon.

A. Yes.

Q. *Let's talk about the first tactic, which is to survive by running away.*

A. Okay. As soon as you realize you're in an active shooter situation, your first thought should be to flee. It should be flight. If you are a moving target, you are almost impossible to hit with a gun. Also, why would you want to stand still, and thus volunteer to be the target of choice in a crowded room?

As you run away, don't run in a straight line. I'm not telling you to serpentine, but you don't want to run in a straight line. With just a little zigzagging, you'll be nearly impossible to hit, and every inch you get further away is an improved chance you have of survival. Distance is your friend.

If you need to hide briefly to get that distance, hide briefly, let him walk past you, and get that distance. If you need to play dead, play dead and get him past you so you can get that distance.

Now, something to keep in mind as you're making the decisions necessary to survive is that if you hide or play dead, you are going to have things that may draw attention to you. Any twitch, any cough, any motion, or your cell phone will draw attention to you.

I'm sure everybody reading this has at some point sat in a restaurant or a bar and noticed that if a television is on, it doesn't matter if it's underwater pottery that's on, you are going to watch it. The mind is programmed to pay attention to whatever is in motion. It's part of the way the human mind works.

If you're going to play dead, you'd better do it well. What is keeping you alive is the motion of others because that's what the shooter's attention will be drawn to. Somebody else will be that target, but it won't be you because you're not drawing attention to yourself, you're not moving.

It's not that you aren't going to be seen or that he's going to be fooled and say, "Oh, I already shot that one," it's that among the 100 or 200 or 300 people in the room, you are not drawing attention.

Q. He's looking for motion. His eye is drawn to motion.

A. Yes. That's what will attract him—motion.

Q. It seems almost cold-hearted and selfish to say that your first goal should be to not draw attention to yourself so that the shooter will focus on someone else. I think most people are going to have a hard time wrapping their minds around the idea that they need to take care of themselves first and that the person next to them may die but that's just the way it has to be.

A. It's the airline rule of "put on your own oxygen mask first" because if you're dead, you can't help anyone else. You hear this on every airline flight: When the oxygen masks drop, put on yours first then help those around you.

That's the mentality here. If you're alive, you're either going to escape and be a witness, or you're going to stay and hopefully be a force for good in thwarting the attack. But you are useless to everybody if you're dead. Put on your mask first, then put on the masks of those around you.

Q. How do you decide if escape is feasible?

A. Earlier we talked about what to do to be ready in case something happens. I said make sure you know where those exits are.

If you know where those exits are, you know your path. Will you be shot if you take them or is the shooter distracted or otherwise occupied? If he's facing south and you're running north, you're adding distance with every step. If he just emptied his magazine and he's putting in a new magazine, you've got three seconds, maybe ten. If the gun jams, you probably have two minutes. You can't count on that happening but it can and it will at times. So there's the potential of several minutes in which you can either oppose or ideally run.

At the same time, what if he decides to go around the corner? He's looking in another room. He's no longer in your presence and he can't see what you're doing, so get out.

I should add another interesting piece to this too. The police will be outside. They'll get there very rapidly after the 911 calls start coming in, and they'll be watching everything happening. They know what they're doing. They are very focused. And do not have in your possession or in your hands anything that could be mistaken for a weapon—and that includes your cell phone—or you may be mistaken for the assailant and suffer friendly fire.

Q. Okay, so your first choice should be to flee, to get out if you can. But you've looked around, and you don't see an opportunity to escape. What should you do and, equally important, what should you not *do?*

A. You should not draw attention to yourself. Do not scream. Do not exhibit broad movements that the shooter will see, or you will become a target.

If you can, get your cell phone out of the picture. It's bad news for you through-and-through. I don't care if you put it in a pocket and you turn it off—and I mean *turn it off!*—just get it out of the situation. If you don't, it will light you up, it will make you buzz, it will play a song, or it will be mistaken for a weapon. *It will draw attention to you time and time again!* Your cell phone is bad news. Get it out of that picture as best you can, as quickly as you can. The more you can keep attention away from yourself, the better the chances you will survive.

Q. I hadn't thought about the potential danger in keeping your cell phone with you and turned on.

A. Within the Pulse nightclub, 202 trigger pulls were engaged to shoot at those 300 people. Mateen continued to shoot the piles of dead bodies. It was a behavior and characteristic we'd never seen before.

We haven't heard people telling about who were flailing their arms around and screaming inside the club. But we've heard a lot about people who were sitting in there as he was hunting for them, calling people, texting people, messaging. Well, if they were doing that, their cell phones were on. If they were doing that, their screens were lit. If they were doing that, their phones were reacting to the inbound calls and messages with buzzes and sounds.

And here's the largest mass shooting in America. Nobody's telling us anybody went around screaming or flailing their arms, but more people died in that incident than any other. Look at the prevalence of cell phone usage; it came out in the media.

Q. So there is a strong possibility, and we may never know for sure, that at the Pulse nightclub there were piles of dead bodies but their phones were ringing and he was shooting at the phones. He didn't know if they were actually dead, he was just shooting at the phones because they were making noise.

A. Very possible. I don't think we'll ever know, but it's very possible.

I'm sure anybody reading this has been in a meeting where suddenly someone's cell phone goes off. If there are 300 people listening to a lecture and one cell phone goes off, every head turns in that direction.

That's not people trying to shoot somebody—it's simply human nature. Now if you're somebody like Mateen, who is standing there looking to kill people, who pulled that trigger 202 times—what is that ringing cell phone going to do for him? "Oh, I missed one." That's what's going through his head. He's already decided he doesn't want anybody walking away, so any noise, any motion will draw the fire.

Now, nowhere have I read that someone was shot because they screamed, ran, whatever. But it sure makes logical sense in the Pulse nightclub shooting when you see those numbers and realize the prevalence of cell phone use throughout the entire attack; there is a very likely correlation.

Q. We have become a culture where, when something happens, it seems that so often our first instinct is to grab the cell phone and hit the video button because we are going to record it. You know, "Oh, my gosh, I'm in the middle of a mass shooting, let me record this and I'll be a YouTube star"—dead, but a YouTube star.

A. Do it if you want to, but leave that phone behind if you do, don't take it with you, because it's going to do other things to draw attention to you. And, by the way, since you're talking about the change of our society, the new social media mentality that's occurring, my wife saw a great expression that she read somewhere: "In case of fire, please exit the building before posting to social media." We are losing that logic to do the important things first. We are losing that thought process, that common sense. And in this type of situation, if you make that mistake, it's a death sentence.

Q. So if you can, drop your phone, drop anything else, and run as far away as you can, as fast as you can.

A. Yes. Before we go further, there's something I want to explain.

Everything that is done by any human being, be it you as a victim, be it him as the shooter, be it law enforcement, goes through something that is known in law enforcement as the OODA loop. Observe, Orient, Decide, Act. You observe, you orient, you decide, you act. You do it over and over, moment by moment by moment. In advancing the pages of this book, you observed your position on the page, oriented where it was relative to the bottom, decided to continue reading, and acted by turning the page. Your own OODA loop engaged. If the phone rang, a child cried, a door knock occurred, or any other distractor took place, you stopped that process. Your own OODA loop was disrupted.

If you can disrupt someone's OODA loop, you disrupt the act. If they can't get to the A in the OODA loop, they can't get to act. So if the shooter is about to do something and you're brave enough to do this, start throwing things at him.

In his OODA loop, he has observed who he's going shoot next. He has oriented where to take the shot. He has decided to pull the trigger and then he's going to pull the trigger and act. If suddenly a 300-pound guy jumps on his back, that trigger won't get pulled. If suddenly a tennis ball hits him upside the head, that trigger won't get pulled. If suddenly a slipper goes past the front of his eyeballs, that trigger won't get pulled. You have the ability to interrupt the OODA loop and stop him from acting. Now, at the same time, you are introducing a motion—

Q. And motion draws attention to yourself.

A. Right. Disrupting the OODA loop is best done in a collective, where several people are taking actions. But if he's aiming that gun at you and you think you're standing there helpless, that there's nothing you can do, here's a great use of your cell phone: Throw it at him and run like crazy.

You just bought yourself three seconds. Put that time to use to gain distance. Make another target more desirable. Jump under, over, behind something. Whatever you can do.

If you have friends and you are all bombarding him with stuff, move back every time you do it. Give yourself a better chance to escape.

You really have to go pretty far into a situation to be out of options, and this is where again, if we go back to Columbine, if we go back to, I believe the Pulse fits, if we go back to Virginia Tech—nobody did these things. There was the opportunity to improve their situation, to escape, and it was missed.

I should also add, in defense of cell phones, that if the shooter is close to you—and especially if he is aiming at you—there is one feature that *might* save your life. More than 90 percent of the information you receive is through your eyes. When that information flow is disrupted, you freeze for several seconds. The stereotypical "parking" scenario where a young couple is making out in a car and a kindly police officer comes by and shines his very bright light in the car is a true demonstration of this effect. The couple is frozen for several seconds while the officer has that time to assess the situation and engage his OODA loop ahead of the couple.

If you can get a shooter blinded with your flashlight feature, then you just bought seconds to change the situation and flee or take cover. It isn't much time, but it's precious time.

Q. Okay, we've talked about fleeing. The second tactic you recommend is defend. What do you mean by that?

A. Okay, you have two major means of killing that have been typically used in this type of situation. The first means is a firearm, the second means is an explosive. Each one has different characteristics. If you are dealing with a firearm, the question you need to ask yourself is: Do you have a place where you can shelter yourself where a bullet will not penetrate?

Penetration mechanics are different for every bullet. Each one has a different depth of penetration into anything you look at as a possible shield. So it's kind of hard to tell you what's what, but, you know, generally, a good thick steel plate is going to work.

Being behind a car is probably going to work, being behind a sheet of drywall is probably not going to work. If the guy wants to get penetration, a bullet may reduce velocity, but for the most part, he is probably going to carry something that will penetrate right through drywall. What about a heavy steel door? What if you are behind a door and you've gotten yourself into the room and can barricade that door with piles of furniture? What are the odds of a bullet getting through?

The other thing to remember is that if you are in a situation where you are forced to hide, be careful because in a shooting incident, the bullet ricochets and finds a path to get to the ground. If it doesn't land inside something, then that means that you're at higher risk if you're lying down. You ideally want to crouch. You want to minimize your exposure on the ground. Don't lie down behind a sofa, crouch behind the sofa—you will be safer against a gun.

Now another thing of concern: What happens if he is not the only assailant?

Q. That's a good point. We've been talking about situations where it's a lone shooter, but it can be two or more.

A. And the oddity is that when they work in pairs or more, the pattern has been that they stay together. So far, at least in the United States, they haven't broken up. However, there have been assaults elsewhere in the world outside the United States where there have been multiple attackers, and they have broken up into smaller groups.

Q. Like the Paris attacks.

A. Yes, and different hotel and shopping mall attacks, where there have been multiple attackers at the same time. So if you have that situation where the shooters have split up, or if you're not sure how many there are, what's important now is that you have to make a decision about what to do.

If you are concerned that there's another one, remember not to be seen through a window. Stay below the window level. Now there are two reasons for that. One is you don't want to be seen from the outside and mistaken for another shooter, or someone another shooter wants to take out. The other reason is the window will now highlight your existence and draw attention to you. Staying below window level with as much mass, as much matter, as many things as you can put between you and any shooters, the stronger and tougher the better—that will let you survive a bullet if it comes your way.

Now again, you're doing a double-down here. You're getting out of the line of sight, you're going into concealment, and you are adding enough mass to survive the shot. You're not drawing attention, but if he sees you, if he decides to engage you, you might still survive. So you are improving your odds over simply being in the room.

Q. *So when we say defend, are we talking about hiding?*

A. Not necessarily. We're talking about four possible levels of response: flee, defend, oppose and defeat. The first one, to flee, is the ideal. You want to escape, to get away.

But there are a lot of situations in which that is just not practical; it can't happen. You may not have a safe exit path, or you may be with someone you don't want to leave. So what do you do? Your next option is to get to a point where you *can* flee. You want to conceal yourself, to protect yourself, to hide until you can safely flee. That's what I mean by defend.

Q. *I see. Let's talk about what you mean by oppose.*

A. Let's say you can't flee and you can't defend. There's no place to go and no place to hide. You're in an open space, and you're too close to the shooter. What can you do?

This is scary stuff, and it's not recommended. What I'm telling you now is for when you have no other choice, these are some tactics to consider.

If you are dealing with a person who has a long gun, grab the barrel. Your hand will burn, but he is holding a long club from a very small end and trying to keep control. Picture a broom. The person holding the end of the broom has little control over it, but if someone else grabs the middle of the broomstick, they can rip the broom away from that person. The same situation applies to a long gun. If you can grab the barrel, I don't care if the shooter is a 300-pound man and you are the class weakling—you now control that gun. He cannot aim. He cannot do anything until you are free of the gun. And any force you apply to take it from him is multiplied by the distance between your grip and his—it all multiplies *your* force in taking the gun away.

If you want to see this principle in action, take a broom and hold it from one end as though it were a gun—whether the bristle end or the other side, and try to stop someone far weaker from you from taking it away. You will fail. The weakest person you know, using their pinky finger alone, will move that broom away. In fact, if you grab it from the side without the bristles, you will find out just how hard it is to hold any straight object with weight on the other end. Those bristles have the same leverage feature, and the combination of their light weight and the distance from your grip at the other end will literally begin to pull apart your grip.

The moment you have ripped that gun away, it is a club that is ready for immediate use. Use it. You do not engage that shooter unless you are as willing to kill him as he was to kill you. This is not a "oh, I'm gonna knock you on the ground and everything will be fine" thing. Beat him with the club until he's incapacitated. If you only knock him out for a few moments, he will kill you when he awakens. You must be vicious in order to survive. He knows he is going to die tonight, and he has accepted that. Be vicious. Make sure you stop him for good. I'm sorry to say that doing so may very well mean killing him.

Q. *So that old "stop or I'll shoot" or "don't come any closer or I'll hit you" thing doesn't apply here.*

A. No. Your life is at stake, and the shooter isn't reading off the same script you are.

You need to use every ounce of your being to defeat that person. In the case of a long gun, he's ready to give you a weapon if you are brave enough to go after it. He is counting on no resistance, so the element of surprise is also on your side.

In most cases, if it's a fish in a barrel situation, they're not aiming, they're just firing. If they *are* aiming, if they're picking up that gun, looking through that gunsight and figuring out who to shoot next at a distance, their attention is very much drawn to one place. In that case, you come up from a different angle. Recognize where that sight is, recognize what he is doing, recognize where his focus is and take advantage of it to the best of your ability. Come up from behind him, from the side, and grab the barrel of his weapon. My hope is nobody ever needs to do this, but if they do, it's an option.

The other thing to keep in mind is the gunman must pull a trigger to kill. Can you stop him? Can you get your finger behind the trigger? Can you jam something in there? Is there something you can do to prevent the trigger pull?

Putting your own finger behind the trigger is a technique that has been used in a few instances. You will break your finger, and you should accept that and know that going in. Your finger will be broken, but you will live to complain about it. And now that weapon is disabled. What's more important, the weapon is yours. He cannot aim it. He cannot shoot it. He also cannot prevent you from pulling it out of his hand as, once again, you have more leverage.

> *During our conversation, we demonstrated these techniques. We used a 12-gauge shotgun, a .38 caliber snub-nosed pistol and a .380 semi-automatic handgun. In each case, I was able to take control of the weapon from a much larger man, whether I did it with my finger behind the trigger or by grabbing the barrel. These methods do work. ~ JL*

If you can't safely get in close to him, then you have a different situation. Ideally, you're not going to want to take this person on by yourself, but you're probably not the only one in fear of their life. If you try and rush somebody, what happens? Some will join you, some will not. Even if the gunman is still in a position to kill, among the crowd, most will reach him, but some will fail. I often compare this to the people who stopped the fourth plane on 9/11. They died, but they did so preventing the killers from achieving their goals. I don't wish anyone to die, but none of us wants everyone to die. What's important now? The risk may be worth taking.

So all of these are options to be able to oppose the shooter and also to defeat the weapon. These are your means of absolute last resort. Don't make them primary unless you absolutely must. Go back to that "what's important now" principle—if you have to disable that shooter because you just have too much at stake in that room and you don't have a choice, those are a few options. You will have more depending on the situation and the setting.

Q. Let's talk about the final tactic, which is to defeat the shooter. This is a good place to also talk about what you should do in an active shooter situation if you happen to be armed.

A. Armed is a pretty broad term. Odds are pretty good you didn't walk into the place carrying a machine gun. But let's say you have a firearm of some type.

Chances are you are carrying something along the lines of a concealed carry weapon, probably something small, a .22 or a 9mm, a .380, a .38. You also would be having a very short barrel in order to carry it concealed. You also probably will not be shooting in a single-action fashion where you can get accuracy. So having that type of weapon means for you to be effective, you have to be close to be accurate. You are not going to successfully fire that weapon and kill the assailant in a roomful of people at a distance of 70 feet. You will kill someone else, and you will spend your life in a jail cell regretting it.

Unfortunately, if he is there with a SIG Sauer MCX like Mateen had at the Pulse nightclub or some other long gun, and you're carrying an easily-concealed handgun, you have to be inside their kill distance to be at your kill distance. You must process that before you take an action. Think that over. The shooter's long gun is more accurate than your tiny gun, and he doesn't care if he hits the wrong person—but you do.

If you are already inside that kill distance, it's an entirely different situation. You don't have to approach, which puts you at great risk in trying to flee. You're already there, so you may be safer engaging and shooting.

Now if you remember at the very beginning of this discussion, we talked about the odd person that sets the hairs up on the back of your neck. He comes in and you decide you can't get away, and I said to stay close. This is especially true if you are armed. By the time they get the long gun up to shoot, you will have your concealed carry weapon pressed against them, and end the situation.

On the other hand, if you are 75 feet away when the shooting starts, you want to be running *away*, not running *to*. That weapon in your pocket or on your belt, whatever, is not going to save you. It may get you in a lot of trouble.

You have to think about what happens in this scenario. Consider what might have happened if a person was armed in the Pulse nightclub. Under Florida law, you cannot have a weapon in an area where alcohol is served. You will go to jail for saving those people. You may decide that's acceptable. You may not. Each state will have a different law. You need to understand that law and how it applies as well.

And that's a scary thing. Each state has a different law for when you draw that firearm or if you can even possess it. Here's a bizarre instance: Philadelphia police were trained that they had to always be on duty and always have their weapon at their side. New Jersey bans the presence of weapons, especially on the beaches. So the police from Philadelphia, who drove a few miles into New Jersey to go to the beach on their day off and followed the Philadelphia police rules, were being arrested in New Jersey for violating New Jersey laws.

Q. That's crazy.

A. But it's the law. The laws are so diverse. If you're going to carry a weapon, you need to know what the laws are wherever you go. If you have to fire your weapon, especially in a mass shooting situation, you will be making a split-second decision, and you'd better be sure you're making the right one.

In Florida, where we're recording this interview, if you have your concealed carry permit, you cannot draw the weapon out of concealment unless human life is at risk. If a guy happened to grab a rabbit and hold a gun to its head, you can't pull your weapon. Human life is not at risk in that situation. If he shot a dog, your weapon stays holstered. If he stole a car, your weapon stays holstered. But if he points a gun at another human being, all bets are off. And every state is different. So know the laws where you are.

Q. What if you have a weapon like a knife?

A. It's the same model. The weapon is only useful to you if you are very close. Guns are often called stand-off weapons because they operate from the distance that you are standing off (or away) from your target. Knives aren't. Yes, you can throw them, but, you know the odds there—good luck.

Q. That's usually only effective in the movies.

A. Right. So, yeah, if you can think you can cut the guy's arm and disable him that way, great, but for you to do it, you have to get within inches of him. Let's say he is sitting there shooting people, or standing there shooting people. So, can you use a knife? Only in certain circumstances. Or once again, if you are suspicious of this person before the shooting starts, you might want to have that knife in your hand and ready to go just in case. Maybe not with the blade exposed—you don't want to look like a threat to others before the freaky person engages. But maybe you want to be ready, so if and when the gun comes out, you're stabbing him in the back.

Q. *Earlier when you mentioned the Luby's Cafeteria massacre, it reminded me of the story of one of the survivors, Dr. Susan Gratia-Hupp. She was having lunch with her parents. She had a gun, but she had left it locked in her car instead of taking it inside the restaurant because she didn't want to risk violating the concealed weapons law. She has spoken publicly and has a YouTube video of that, talking about reaching for her weapon but then remembering that it was in her car. Both of her parents were killed.*

A. I've actually eaten at that Luby's in Killeen. It's an odd experience picturing the truck in the middle of the room, with the two 9mm guns firing at everyone. They rebuilt the place with a lot of brick at the base to prevent the incident from happening again, but Luby's no longer operates that location today. Dr. Gratia-Hupp's concealed handgun would not have been a match for the shooter unless he was shooting elsewhere or otherwise distracted, enabling her to shoot him. And that could have happened, as he reloaded three times, but it also may have been impossible since he also had the cover of his truck.

Again, he did not care who he killed with a missed shot, but she did. The odds of success were against her even if she had her gun. But notice that the lessons of the Luby's massacre are the same—one patron broke through a window, allowing others to place distance between them and the shooter. The shooter killed 23, injured 27, but more than 250 escaped with their lives. He also was focused mainly on killing women—he had identified his target group and was selective. The incident ended with him committing suicide when injured by police. The same scenario that we keep observing applied here—no resistance despite three reloads, and the shooter ending up dead; however, those who were able to flee survived.

Q. So let's say you decide to attack the attacker because that's the only option you have. You've got a group—whether you're going to just throw things or actually going to jump on him and take him down—what are some tips for communicating to the other people about what you want to do? Because maybe you are the only person who read this book, maybe you're the only person who's thinking, "Okay, this is what we need to do." How do you get people working with you?

A. The first thing to remember is anybody will do what they're trained to do. The possible reactions of anybody reading this book are probably being changed by this book. They're going to think differently now; they're going to act differently. But they're going to be surrounded by people, at least in the near term, who still think the old way, which is "let's hide."

Now, when the Virginia Tech shooting began and the students sat at their desks—I don't know how they would have communicated with each other. They probably could have said to each other. "Let's mob him." Maybe they could have convinced him to run out of that classroom and move on to the next, I don't know. Maybe they could have said, "Let's all run through the door" and 50 percent would have survived. It still would have been better than the number who did survive.

Or talking about the Colorado movie theater. I don't know that the people sat in their seats. I suspect they probably got down on the floor as close as they could behind the seats. I'm hoping they had the sense to do that. If that is what they did, then at that point they could make their pact amongst themselves to do something. But remember, you have shooting, you have screaming. You don't want to yell to each other and have the assailant hear you.

Q. *And hear what you are planning to do.*

A. And draw attention to yourself. A whisper might not work. So the bottom line is, you're going to have to decide what fits the situation you're in.

In the Pulse nightclub, there was very loud music in the initial moments, then that was turned off. So now, what we are aware of? We have some amazing insights from all that cell phone traffic. We know where the people were hidden because they stayed on their cell phones and kept talking to each other. They were sending out targets to him. He knew where people were alive. There were noises going on. He knew. So he was able to focus.

On the other hand, they had found a way to communicate also with each other. Had they desired to oppose him, they could have come up with a plan. In my mind, reading the reports of the Pulse, I saw people who simply hid in rooms. They didn't think about barricading doors. They didn't think about becoming a united force. They did not think about letting him come through a door and then slamming it on his arm and beating the tar out of him before he could get any further in the room. They did not think about opposing; they thought about calling for help or calling loved ones to say goodbye.

So once again, what do you do? *What's important now?*

A crowded movie theater is going to be one dynamic. Whether a film was being shown, whether the lights were on or off, those things would change the best way to handle that.

In a crowded bar, the music is playing loud, forget it. Good luck communicating with each other. On the other hand, if it's quiet except for screams and gunshots, you may be able to make hand gestures with enough light and get people going.

Again, what is the situation and how do you address it? And it's right back to that "What's important now?" Look at your environment and make that decision.

And remember United Airlines Flight 93, the jet that never reached its target on 9/11. The passengers did conspire to stop the attack, and they succeeded by crashing the plane in a field in Pennsylvania. They communicated their final decision with a mere two words that *every* American of driving age understands clearly: "Let's roll!" There are always ways to communicate, and many are swift or silent. If you need to find those words, you will. "Get him!" certainly conveys the point just as well.

Realize, too, that we have a very polarizing set of positions on guns, and the lack of ability to discuss them leaves many with false impressions. A fully automatic weapon, which fires many rounds with each trigger pull, is a very rare thing and restricted substantially. To my knowledge, never has an automatic weapon been used in an active shooter event. A semi-automatic weapon is very common—this means that after each trigger pull, the (typically brass) casing is ejected from the gun and another bullet put into the chamber. It's one trigger pull per bullet. A standard pistol (often called a revolver for its revolving chamber) revolves its chamber after each shot to have another live bullet in the chamber.

If the crowd believes that fully automatic weapons are in place—and many people believe this due to the film industry and inaccurate media coverage after killings—then they will believe the gun to have more capability than it possesses. The media and politicians now talk about assault weapons and assault-style weapons.

If you dig through the rhetoric, an "assault-style" weapon has one or more features that make it *look like* an assault weapon. However, the true distinction is that an assault weapon is not sold to John Q. Public, and is intended for warfighting—it shoots many rounds per trigger pull. The Sig Sauer MCX used at Pulse and the Armalite Rifle weaponry (AR-4, AR-15, AR-16) used at other sites were *not* automatic weapons. The bullets were fired one at a time, not in a spray.

But if people believe a spray could come out, they will see no time to save their lives. If they understand that there is a delay between each trigger pull, then their understanding of their options changes. Unfortunately, the dialogue has been killed in favor of agendas and the lack of accurate information is hurting our citizens. This misinformation will make them more paralyzed, more fearful and more hesitant to engage a shooter.

All of these factors will play into the minds of those around you. You may find your best move is to lead by example. Tell them "Let's roll!" or "Get him!" and then immediately lead the charge.

Q. We've talked about playing dead, and you said that if you need to do it short-term, do it just to give yourself time to look for an escape opening. Let's talk about why you shouldn't play dead.

A. The biggest risk for you when you play dead is being hit by a weapon brought in by the assailant. We haven't gone into the bombs yet, we've stayed with guns. If the assailant's gun is in proximity to you, then you are still at risk. When you flee, you're out of range. You are no longer at risk.

So if you consider this from simply a risk abatement perspective, standing up next to the gunman waiving your hands and saying, "Hi, shoot me," is a lot more dangerous than running away from him in a zigzag pattern and escaping. Playing dead falls in between those two extremes.

Think about which is less dangerous: Is it safer to get out of range of his weapon or is it safer to lie down next to him, waiting for him to step on you for you to scream, "Ouch!" or for the person next to you who is also playing dead to cough or move? If anything happens to draw his attention *near* you, then you can count on a hailstorm of bullets coming your way. When do you have the least risk, the greatest chance of safety? Whenever there is distance between you and the shooter. Distance is your greatest friend. If you can do it, you want the distance.

If you can't do it immediately, you want to seize the opportunity to do it as soon as you can. And if you can't do it because there's somebody in that room you cannot leave, then you've got a whole new set of priorities to figure out. Playing dead is not a good idea for the long term. You may have a chance at survival, but you are not increasing your odds of doing so. All you're doing is waiting out the situation.

And if we go back to the Pulse nightclub again, at the end he started shooting the bodies. He started shooting the dead again. There were stories about those who were playing dead who got shot and survived. Now, what we haven't heard, and I don't know this answer: Why did he shoot them again? Did he still have bullets and hatred and wanted just to shoot at dead bodies? Did a cell phone go off? Did a person cough? Did a stomach rumble?

Q. Were there not other people still moving around that he could have shot?

A. Exactly. Why would his attention have drawn back to the dead? Either there was no one else to shoot or something re-attracted him to the targets on the ground. Again, maybe a cell phone, a rumbling stomach, a hiccup, a cough, a sob.

By the way, if you're playing dead, you're just part of the pile. He may take you out without even you doing a thing to draw the attention, because the person next to you may have done something. If we are dealing with a stack of bodies, what if a dead one simply falls? That will attract his attention. He will shoot again. You happen to be next to that body, I'm sorry, but gravity will have made you a target.

Q. Most of what we've been talking about so far seems to apply if the shooter is on the same physical level that you are, in the same room or general area. What about the situation in

Las Vegas, where the shooter was on the 32nd floor of the Mandalay Bay? We've heard many stories of people who apparently knew what to do and got themselves and others out of harm's way, but I'm sure there were plenty of people who survived by chance and not because of any purposeful action. What can you do in a situation like that, when you're in a crowd and someone is shooting down into it, either rapidly spraying bullets of shooting people one at a time as a sniper?

A. What's important to note here is not just that the situation you described is different from, for example, Virginia Tech, but that the tactic is different. "Kill box" is a term the military uses to describe the area where all the munitions are aimed in a battle. The term has been casually reapplied to the civilian sector at times to describe a scenario where fire is directed to a given region that has trapped personnel inside of it. The term was also used in the *Iron Man 2* film when the two heroes were in a position below all the surrounding areas, and thus in a kill box.

The distinction you make is correct for Las Vegas, but realize that it also applied to the Manchester bombing and to the Pulse nightclub in Orlando. In those situations, you had a large congregation of people with minimal ability to escape. They were effectively all positioned inside a "box" where they could be killed en masse—hence, a "kill box."

This discussion is relatively new territory, and the terms we use today may rapidly become outmoded, but let's separate the two events. The "kill box" scenario is certainly distinct from the other scenarios but is not limited to the existence of someone on a different vertical level. The Pulse nightclub event still had a kill box, as only one point of egress was available to the victims, and the shooter had blocked it. The people were trapped in a box, and thus it was a kill box scenario. So let me suggest that we discuss the scenarios as "boxed" and "unboxed." I have no doubt that new terms will emerge soon and require another update.

Q. *Sadly, I'm sure you're correct. For now, we'll add those terms in this context to our vocabularies.*

A. We covered the unboxed scenario earlier. In an unboxed situation, you have options. Some of those options still fit a boxed scenario. The applications change, though.

In an unboxed scenario, the shooter will likely take aim at individuals at close range. In a boxed scenario, the shooter will take aim at whatever concentration of people catches his eye and he'll attack from an extended distance. The ideal countermeasure for both situations is to go unnoticed.

Many years ago, the U.S. Army published a concept for vulnerability that may apply well here. I don't recall it perfectly, but I can adapt it to this subject matter:

1) Don't be detected.
2) If detected, don't be seen.
3) If seen, don't be shot.
4) If shot, don't be killed.

That approach fits both boxed and unboxed scenarios. If the shooter does not take notice of you—or, in the case of the boxed scenario, of those near you—then you will not be detected. If you are detected, then you don't want to be an obvious target. The shooter will go for the most obvious targets first. If you can be seen, then do your best to have something between you and the shooter so you can't be shot.

Protect yourself to the extent possible so that you can't be killed, even if you are shot.

We've already talked about the Pulse nightclub situation, so let's clarify that for the Las Vegas situation. A huge crowd was being fired upon. They didn't know at first that shots were being fired, nor could they initially tell the direction of fire. Let's come at this from the perspective of someone in that crowd.

In a boxed scenario, the first victims do not have the advantage of knowing that there is a shooting before the bullets strike. With that in mind, their best move would have been to consider their placement at the event. However, even if they planned for the unknown event, the shots could have come from any direction, so their options were few. At most events, the desire is to have the best view. While that makes for the greatest enjoyment of the event, it also places you in the center of mass for the crowd. I can't tell you what is more important—your enjoyment or your preparation. It's your decision. In the vast majority of situations, there won't be a shooter. But if you believe in your gut that something is wrong and want to take precautions, then be away from the center of the crowd and near some obstacle or exit. I'm the person giving you this information and will tell you personally that I'd still go for the view unless my gut was really off the charts. Don't sacrifice life's enjoyment in the fear of losing life, but listen to your body and soul.

Now the shots begin. We are in the crowd. Initially, we don't know what those loud popping sounds are. There is an echo that prevents us knowing where they are coming from. Until people fall or someone yells that it's a shooting, we are still clueless. And in a large, dense, noisy crowd, it's possible that even after people fall, even after someone yells, we may still not know what's happening but we might sense that something is wrong. So what should we do?

Moving away from the largest pockets of the crowd is a good idea, but you are at ground level and can't tell where they end. To move away from the crowd also makes you alone in an open space that may make you an easy target.

Forgive me, but welcome to hell. There is no clear and simple answer at this time since you don't know for sure what's happening. To survive, you want to drop below the height of the crowd, but to learn what is going on, you want to rise above the height of the crowd to gain information.

My best advice to you is to realize that at this moment in time you will hear more than you will see and you won't lose information if you make yourself shorter. Do not get onto the ground, but conceal your head below the height of the crowd. Remember: *"If detected, don't be seen."* From the shooter's vantage point, you no longer exist, and the group around you is one member smaller, deserving slightly less interest for the shooting. If you tell those around you to also get down lower, you again reduce the size of the target to the shooter (and you reduce the exposure to vital organs, adding safety to you and reducing the interest of the shooter in firing in your direction). You do not need to sacrifice others to save yourself.

Next, we figure out that there is a shooting occurring. Our head is down. If we are in a crowd and not exposed, we are not safe, but we are not likely to be the one hit. Now we can think and try to figure out where the shots are coming from. Just as in the unboxed scenario, distance is our friend. Escape if possible, but if escape isn't possible, we want to find the safest possible way to put distance between ourselves and the shooter.

Why? Let's get into some of the physics of the situation. In order to hit you specifically, a shooter at a great distance must target you, account for gravity's pull, account for wind impacts on the munitions, and figure out where you will be exactly while you are in motion. As distance increases, he can't be off target by even a fraction of a fraction of an inch or he will miss you completely. Also, the bullet he is shooting is losing velocity as it flies through the air, making it a gradually less-lethal bullet.

To understand these effects, first, take a laser pointer (ideally) or a flashlight. Point it at a distant wall (even inside your home). Notice how little you need to move the light on your end to create a huge change in position at the other end. The greater the distance, the greater the change in impact point from a tiny movement at the point of origin. You adding distance forces the shooter to add accuracy—which takes time. He'd rather find another pocket of people.

Just as distance is our friend, we also must remember the *"don't be seen"* piece. That trendy bright yellow outfit will draw attention a lot faster than anything drab. If you have a way to reduce your attention-grabbing features, then use it. The shooter is trying to spray bullets to kill people in numbers. The less you look like the next Hollywood starlet and the more you look like an oddly moving rock, the better your chances of not drawing fire.

As you move away, also pay attention to your surroundings. A portable toilet won't protect you ballistically, but it will conceal your existence. He won't be shooting portable toilets, but he will be looking for groups of people. Get behind anything you can. If the object can protect you ballistically—that is, if it can reduce the ability of the bullet to reach you with full force—that's even better.

Ballistic protection here is not the same as we would discuss for military or law enforcement but is simply the existence of something that will thwart the bullet's ability to kill you. The bullet, when fired, will have mass (its weight), velocity (its speed), trajectory (its course), shape (a pointed item ready to penetrate upon impact), and spin (which keeps the bullet flying straight). All of these features combine to make a bullet lethal. Take some of them away and you have achieved some level of simple ballistic protection.

The portable toilet won't do much beyond slightly slowing the bullet, as the plastic walls are thin and won't do much to the bullet. However, a surface of steel, concrete, or even wood have far more effect. Further, a layered set of materials—think about a trailer wall with metal outside, insulation inside it, and then a drywall or wood panel inside—will greatly affect the bullet.

Let's take this line by line:

Mass. You can't do much here. The bullet will weigh what it weighs.

Velocity. The moment a bullet goes through something besides air, it loses velocity. Every change in its environment slows it down. Water slows it significantly, which is why being behind a fountain is still useful. Steel may stop it completely. Every impact with a new surface that the bullet makes reduces its velocity—and thus its energy.

Trajectory. The bullet's trajectory will shift slightly each time it changes what it's penetrating. So when a bullet hits something, even though it's continuing to move, it's no longer on its original course.

Shape and spin. If the bullet remains a round, pointed object that's in its original shape, it's going to fly straight and accurately. If it hits anything that crushes it or makes it imperfect, then it begins to tumble in the air and loses velocity and trajectory in the process. Think about the bullet passing through that trailer wall we discussed. The bullet's tip will become more and more crushed with each hard surface that it passes through, and that means that it will no longer have a point—it will be like a metal mushroom flying through the air. If the head is no longer pointed, the bullet can't penetrate as effectively. If the bullet is no longer symmetrical, it can't spin properly. It transforms swiftly from a bullet to a flying pebble. It can still hurt, but its ability to kill is severely diminished. It's also slowing rapidly, and thus becoming less lethal in that way as well.

Q. So once you figure out that a shooting is happening, you want to reduce your visibility and put as much distance as possible between yourself and the shooter. What next?

A. Next, you want to escape the area. As I watched the footage from Las Vegas, I noticed the impact of fear and confusion on those who did escape. I really felt for them—they had saved their own lives while knowing that they left others behind. I hope they can realize that their first priority was to save their own lives and that they succeeded. They could not change the world within that "box"—they just had to get out of it. They did the right thing.

I also noticed that many simply fled down the center of a path of egress. It made me wonder about the very techniques that we just discussed. They did put distance between themselves and the shooter—good! They may not have realized it, but there were obstacles between the shooter and them—high poles and gear, and some structures. But they also stayed out in the open. I would have suggested to them that they cling to the exit walls—be less of an easy target and put more mass between them and the shooter. However, kudos to them all. They succeeded. They survived.

Q. *Right. The goal is to survive.*

A. Now that we've covered what to do, let's remember what *not* to do. In the box scenario, we can go back to that repurposed Army statement:

1) Don't be detected.
2) If detected, don't be seen.
3) If seen, don't be shot.
4) If shot, don't be killed.

That statement tells us what not to do. Let's go through it.

Don't be detected. Don't stand out. Don't be a living embodiment of a traffic cone, sunrise, or neon billboard. Don't draw attention to yourself. Don't be dancing, jumping, or standing atop a podium or car. Do your best to blend into the environment so you don't draw attention or fire. If you're wearing a hat, take it off. Remove any other brightly-colored, attention-getting clothing or accessories that you can. Toss them aside and move away from them—your life is more important. Or find a tarp, a blanket, a trash bag, a sweater that turns you into something far less visible and wear it.

Don't be seen. Even if you're dressed to match the pavement beneath your feet, don't be the one standing tall, at the head of the line, or wandering outside the group. Be the invisible person who is just part of the crowd but ideally ducked down below the height of the crowd.

Don't be shot. Don't ignore potential cover around you. Get behind anything solid that will change that shiny sharp bullet from a lethal penetrator into a tumbling mushroom. Find cover, stay low, and get to a protected place.

Don't be killed. Don't lose your wits. Absolutely do not put yourself in a position to be trampled or crushed. *Do not lie down!* If you do, not only will someone likely walk on you, which could seriously injure or even kill you, you will also increase your odds of being struck by a bullet. Remember, gravity pulls on bullets. They usually end up in a wall or on the ground. You don't want your full body on the ground because a bullet, even a slow-moving one, will likely impact you. Keep your exposure to the ground limited to your own two feet. You can duck. You can crouch. But don't lie down.

Q. This is all good advice for a situation like the one in Las Vegas where there was a shooter, but what about when there's a bomb in a crowded venue?

A. Good question. Let's use the Ariana Grande concert in Manchester as an illustration. No one knew the bomb existed until it detonated. Everything was too late from the moment the event began.

This is where all the kill box scenarios come together. Can you plan for the unknown?

Concerts often have assigned seating, so you are where you are. However, there are some things you can do to protect yourself that apply to any scenario.

First, pay attention. Look for anything that seems out of place. If you see something, notify the venue's staff or authorities. Think about how to place something between you and the odd item, such as a steel beam or a support column. If something is making you uncomfortable, you may want to watch the concert from somewhere other than the comfort of your assigned seat. If something is out of place, it may be lethal. Yes, odds are more likely that it's a bag of donuts that someone is planning to enjoy after the event, but the possibility of lethality exists.

Second, plan your escape routes. We'll talk more about this, but for now what's important is that you to know in advance how you're going to get out of a place if you need to.

Third, remember what's important. You probably aren't at this event alone. You're likely with others, possibly your children, parents, or close friends. Think about how you will get them to those exits and to safety.

If you fear an explosive incident, you should also understand just a little bit about explosive effects. If you place an explosive in the middle of an open space, it will generally emit a blast upwards and outwards all 360 degrees. If it's not evenly shaped—not symmetrical—it will burst in a pattern determined by its shape and its weakest point. However, if you place that same explosive against a hard material, then the blast will be reflected by that hard material. Picture a 50-gallon drum of gasoline exploding. If it sits in an open field, it pretty much goes everywhere—throwing the fuel, flame, and compression wave (blast wave, shock wave) in all directions.

If it sits against a concrete or steel wall, then the force of the blast is directed away from that wall and the fuel, flame, and compression wave all approach double intensity on the side opposite that wall.

Q. Why is that important to know?

A. Consider a concert in a multi-tiered stadium-style venue. If that same drum sits inside the seating area, the blast will be blown upwards by the floor and downwards by the ceiling. The explosive yield will be substantial inside that contained "box" area in which you are sitting as the explosive yield is the same (same blast, same flame, same fuel, same fragmentation), but now it will be trapped inside a contained area, and have a greater lethal effect for those within that box. The effects may carry a few more boxes to each side, but the floor and ceiling will likely keep the blast contained to that level and those boxes. So hiding behind a pole or support column within that box will not save you unless you can get totally separated from the source of the blast. You need more distant cover.

By comparison, if the explosive is found in an open area away from your box, then your box may offer you a lot of protection. Where will the blast focus? To contemplate the effects of a blast, think in terms of a giant water balloon getting stepped on. The water is being forced out in all directions except the direction of the shoe squashing it. If that bomb were a giant water balloon, where would the water go? If you can figure out where you won't get wet, then you have most likely figured out where you will survive the blast.

Q. Anything else?

A. Remember your hearing. If you are convinced that a blast is coming, then not only is distance your friend, so is anything that reduces your exposure to the blast. Your ears will still be vulnerable even if you protect yourself from all the effects of the shock wave and debris. Cover them if you can—press the flaps on your outer ear into the canal to seal the ear canal from the shock wave.

CHAPTER FIVE

When Do You Call 911?

Question: *Something we haven't talked about yet is calling 911. How and when does that happen in all of this, with things likely happening so fast?*

Answer: Again, remember the "What's important now?" principle. If you have the opportunity to do it, do it. But let's be honest, what's going to happen? The police are wanting to know where you are, who you are, what's happening. And you don't want to be carrying that cell phone with an active shooter in the room.

I will tell you what the officer said to me when I got my concealed carry permit because this applies in this situation as well as a home break-in. Call the police, tell them what's happening, where it is, who you are and give them your description. You don't even have to do that last one in an active shooter event. They will have a million more questions for you that you don't have the time to answer. So just put the phone down and let them hear everything. You are now away from the cell phone; it's not going to light up and go dark, light up and go dark, attracting attention. It's not going to light you up. It's not going to be an attraction to the assailant—and thus it becomes a distraction, drawing his attention away from you—but you are feeding constant information to the police.

If you listen to what happened at Columbine in the re-enactment, one of the students called 911, began talking to the dispatcher and then called one of the assailants by name. The dispatcher kept calling the assailant [Andre' – which is not the real name of the assailant but was substituted for Eric in the re-enactment] to try and get him on the phone, calling his name through the cell phone. Because the phone connection was open, the police were aware of when shots were fired. They were aware of when the assailants knew the police were there. They heard their comments about the police arriving. They heard where they planned to go next because that cell phone was there pumping out information. They even heard them plan their suicides and decide how to count down before pulling their triggers on themselves together.

So again, don't cling to the cell phone. If you have the opportunity to call 911, do it, and set the phone somewhere where it can just keep giving them data. Don't keep it with you.

In a kill box event, the rules are similar. Can the shooter be attracted by your cell phone? If so, then don't use it. As we discussed earlier, the shooter will be drawn to motion, lights, possibly even sounds. You don't want to draw his attention, so don't. The police will be called—we hope by someone who escapes or an external witness, but likely by someone in the kill box. The 911 dispatchers will probably be flooded with calls. You can call when you feel safe, or when you feel invisible, but don't endanger yourself needlessly.

CHAPTER SIX

What Do You Do When Law Enforcement Arrives?

Question: The arrival of law enforcement on the scene doesn't mean that everything is automatically okay and everyone is safe. Let's talk about what to do so that you help rather than hinder the police.

Answer: As they come in, they will typically be in teams of about three or four and wearing body armor. As they enter the building, you want to simply run past them in the direction of the entrance they took to get in and get out of there. They're there to take out the assailant. They don't want you between them and him. They want you out of the picture.

Q. And once you're outside, there will be other officials who are going to help you if you're injured and deal with you for debriefing.

A. When they can. But first, they need to stop the assailant.

I'm going to tell you the real rules police want you to follow, and I'm going to walk through why. First, as you're running out, don't stop and tell them where the shooter is.

Q. *Why?*

A. Because what have you done to that officer's OODA loop? You've disrupted it.

You have an armed force coming in, possibly with automatic weapons, probably with body armor, looking for the assailant. There's typically going to be four of them, and there's probably another team right behind them. They are creating an overwhelming force to oppose the assailant. They need to stay focused on that.

Remember that I said that only one or two percent of these assailants ever walk out alive. They go in usually knowing they're going to die. When the police show up, they know it's over. So don't try to help the cop coming in—get out of his way, that's how you help him. Run right past them, get out of the way. Because if you stand there and talk to them, then you become the next victim. What's his next choice? If he gets shot talking to you, what have you done to the situation? Do not stop, do not engage them, leave.

When you get outside, and you are out of the danger zone, that's when you can stop. Yes, you just went through a trauma. You are going to be shaking beyond belief, and you are going to find comfort among the others who have gone through it with you. You'll find each other. And eventually when they are ready to deal with the witness statements, law enforcement will find you, and it won't be hard for them to do so. You will stand out from the bystanders.

CHAPTER SEVEN

What Should You Do When You Get Outside?

Question: *Let's talk about the best-case result of the worst-case scenario—you've managed to escape. What do you do once you're outside, once you've reached safety?*

Answer: Get out of the incident zone and be approachable by police.

As you're leaving, as you're running, you don't want to make any sudden movements that could be misconstrued by police. Keep your hands visible. You don't want to be carrying anything that could be perceived as a weapon. If you're carrying a purse, who cares? That's not seen as a weapon. But if you're carrying a cell phone in a dark, crazy environment with a lot of red and blue lights flashing, that may look like a handgun.

Q. *I also want to say to leave the purse or the bags or backpacks. There's nothing in them that you can't replace.*

A. That's absolutely fine, but the point is, don't be mistaken for one of the shooters or it can go badly. If you go out with your hands up, fine. If you go out, just run for your life. You are not showing a threat to anyone. If you're not showing a weapon, no one's going to be attacking you.

Now, since we brought that up, let's remember one other thing too: If you do attack that assailant, and you got possession of the gun, don't hold him at bay with it. We've already talked about this, but I can't stress it enough. You want him out of the picture, and you want that gun either under your foot or away from everybody. Do not pick up that gun and hold him at gunpoint, because when the police come in, they'll see you as the assailant, and you will be taken out. It is pretty much guaranteed.

CHAPTER EIGHT

How Should You Respond to Questions from the Shooter?

Question: *I have heard reports that some shooters have engaged their victims by asking them questions—often about their faith—and then either shooting or not shooting them based on their answers.*

Answer: That has happened overseas, but I'm not aware of it ever happening in the United States.

Q. One of the Columbine shooters asked one of the victims if she believed in God.

A. There is an amazing reenactment of Columbine using the actual sounds from 911 calls. You can type "Columbine Reenactment" into your web browser to find this video, but realize that it is very graphic and disturbing. If you watch that, you'll realize that the victims' faith was not part of the overall issue. They were there to kill indiscriminately. Think, too: they had propane bombs that they were using as part of the attack. They were not interested in specific targets. They were interested in killing as many as possible. Now, overseas what has happened, is you have had Islamic extremist terrorists attack individual hotels and figure out the faith of people and determine who they wish to execute. So it can happen.

What has happened is that demonization process we discussed. The shooter has demonized a certain group in his mind. Let's suppose the Pulse attack really was about the LGBT community. Would Mateen have gone in and started to ask people, "Who are you here with?" or "Are you gay?"

If he was actually targeting the LGBT community, in his head he would have hated only members of that community. If that had been the case, they would have been his only targets. He would have had to filter. But he didn't do that.

Most mass shooters don't do that. Most of them decide to just attack en masse because they hate everybody at the targeted location. If they have created the structure within which they wish to send a political message or they have a specific hatred in mind, they will have to filter. That's when you'll have an interview.

What's your best answer? The one that doesn't lead to the trigger being pulled. I don't know how else to say it.

I don't want to sit here and say, "Go ahead and lie," I leave it up to you. Once again, put on your own mask first. If you can survive, you will be a witness or you will thwart the attacker. I think God will forgive me if I told them that I was something other than what I am to survive a mass shooting and save the lives of others.

Q. I agree with you, but I know there are people who don't. Do you want to talk about when it's okay and not okay to deny your faith?

A. Sure, let's go down that path. In an active shooter situation, you are under the most extreme duress of your existence. You have a duty to serve God in the custom of your faith, whatever that may be. You will not do that very well lying dead on the ground.

Q. I think there is a difference when we talk about denying your faith when you're doing it for a personal or material type of gain, versus doing what you need to do to stay alive to help other people. And if we are wrong, we'll deal with it later—that's between the individual and God.

A. Your life or your faith will not be defined in the ten seconds you spend in front of a gun. That is not what will define your faith. Your lifetime and service to your fellow man will define your faith.

Q. What about other types of questions a shooter might ask, such as where specific people are. I heard that one of the Sandy Hook teachers saved children's lives by saying they weren't in the room when she'd hidden them in a closet. Do workplace violence shooters ask about the location of specific people they want to target?

A. I don't recall that from the Sandy Hook event, but shooter Lanza was a particularly vile killer even among his peers, as he was willing to kill innocent children en masse after killing his own mother. Yet again, the event ended with him committing suicide once faced with opposition from the police.

A mass killer wants to kill as many as possible. Unless he has a specific person or group in mind as a target, there won't be an interview, as the desire to kill everyone will take out the person rather than interview them.

If he is asking, then he has a specific target. The best thing to do is what we said before: What's important now? Tell him to go away from you and get to safety yourself. Try to keep him away from others. If you are nearby, get him refocused away from you and take control of his weapon, calling for others to help. What you say or how you answer is not something of great concern—how you manage the situation and change near-certain death into a chance for life is what matters.

CHAPTER NINE

How Do Multiple Shooters Operate?

Question: Let's talk a little more about the dynamics when there are multiple shooters. How do they operate during the attack? You've said that they tend to stay together.

Answer: Again, the Columbine recreation is very educational on that. The shooters walked from place to place together. They committed suicide together. Everything they did, they did together. That is the general model.

Now, because of the definition I used of active shooter, where I said that it was somebody with a firearm desiring to kill multitudes of people, that means that a terrorist attack is that way too. Terrorists have been known to send teams into hotels to kill people. They've been known to use large-scale weapons and large-scale bombs. They recently drove a van into a crowd and shot people from multiple sides of the van.

Their tactics are very on-purpose. They want to get the maximum killing. They want to make sure that what they do at a low cost to them results in a high cost to their opposition.

So the rule of thumb is that teams or groups stay close together during an event. However, the terrorist methods may vary from this approach. Also remember that the domestic mass shooter typically wants to kill, whereas the terrorist wants to kill, send a message and bankrupt us.

At the risk of digressing, let's consider the terrorist tactics. Do you know how many billions have we spent to prevent the next $45 shoe bomber? There's a mentality to this that is going on and the terrorists bank on it—some call it the death of a thousand cuts. The terrorists find low-cost ways to threaten us, and even if they don't work, we will outspend them millions of dollars to one to prevent their latest device from being used. We now take off our shoes at nearly 20,000 airports—every one of them checking every shoe of every person in line. Why? The device the shoe bomber had cost about $45 dollars and didn't even work. But for us to chase it costs millions.

So terrorists will deliberately rotate their tactics to incorporate new devices, even if those devices don't work. So long as we ignore the individuals and chase the devices, there will always be a new device used. We will always react and never get ahead until we chase the people.

Of course, terrorists also periodically pull off a multiple geography attack. When one of these happens, do you call it one attack or not? On 9/11, was the World Trade Center and the Pentagon one attack or was it a multiple attack? You can see it either way.

The two towers could be considered separate, so you can say that the terrorists stayed together or you can say that they broke apart. The thing is that they made a plan. In that case, the plan was to kill large numbers of people through dramatic means.

When you are dealing with the lone solo shooter or the shooter and his friend or the shooter and his fellow victim who got angry, you are dealing with two or three. You'll know how many you have because the active shooters tend to stay together. When you're dealing with a large-scale terrorist incident, it's a whole new game that's beyond the scope of this conversation. The agenda is broader (ideology, desire for media attention, desire to show power against the nation), the weaponry is more diverse, and the killing may be timed to that agenda. Remember the many bus bombings overseas that waited for the media and law enforcement to show up before blowing up the buses. The media attention may be the more desirable effect for them.

Once again, though, your principles should be the same. What's important now? Get away if you can. Hide if you have to. If you're on the second floor, then a broken leg from jumping out a window or off a balcony may be preferable to a gunshot or explosive blast. If you're in a hotel room, and you've heard shots, then it may be best to lock the door and then barricade it with every piece of furniture you have. The gunshots will be less likely to reach you, and the terrorists don't want to waste time on you when there is a corridor full of other doors to attack. They may fill your door with bullets, but if you're hiding in the steel bathtub and their bullets are penetrating a steel door, a dresser, a mattress, a box spring, and a nightstand, your odds of survival are pretty well increased.

Pay attention and figure out how and when to flee, or if you should stay put in your mini-fortress. There may be bombs, but there may not. Do what you believe is the most important thing at each moment, and your odds of survival will skyrocket.

CHAPTER TEN

What Weapons are the Attackers Using?

Question: *When we say "active shooter," we tend to think primarily of someone with a gun or guns of some type. But we've had perpetrators who have used other types of weapons—knives, machetes, explosives, vehicles and you mentioned drones when we first started talking about this.*

Answer: The use of drones is beginning overseas, it'll be here eventually for the Islamic extremist terrorists.

Q. *So let's talk about those situations where weapons other than guns are used. The Boston Marathon bombers used explosives exclusively. I don't know that there was anything anyone could have done to prevent the bombs from detonating—*

A. Wrong. Horribly wrong. This goes to our culture again.

Q. *Okay. Explain that.*

A. First, let's talk again about what an explosive is, and anybody reading the book can do this, too: Take your two index fingers and tap them together. That is the sound of skin hitting skin. Now clap. That's an explosion.

An explosion is a sudden equalization of pressure. So what is going to explode? Any kind of a vessel holding something that will rapidly expand: Gasoline, when you ignite it, vegetable oil that is heated when you ignite it, propane, any flammable liquid will do that, flammable gases will do that. If you can ignite them, they will blast, and they will create an explosion.

In the Boston Marathon bombing, what they did was, they not only put that together so that the explosion would take place, but they added the fragmentation to it by adding nails into it, so that the nails would be propelled by the blast.

Now, the reason I said "wrong" is this is another problem we have. If we go into a facility and there is something there that we don't expect or understand, we ignore it. This is why you hear officials say over and over again, "If you see something, say something."

If you have a situation where you were to walk into a gym and in a far corner is a gun bag, a rifle bag, a gym bag, a propane tank with wires sticking out of it—what percentage of people do you think would report it? "Oh, gee, he came out of nowhere with a gun!" That would be the end story. No one will report it.

So now, go back to the Boston Marathon. No question about two pressure cookers sitting on the ground in unattended backpacks?

Many of the places you go into today—office buildings, government buildings, airports—an unattended bag will be detonated. A sturdy metal cover will be put over it, and it will be detonated. If there's no explosive, it won't "go boom," but something will go in to charge it and force it to detonate in a controlled condition. That is how real this threat is.

Yet you walk into an auditorium, a gymnasium, a church, a hall of worship, you walk into a school building, and that might not happen. Why do we still ignore what's out of place? Haven't we learned? There *is* something you can do. If you see something and it looks odd, say something to an official. I have watched officials go up and say, "Whose bag is this?" and if it wasn't claimed it's getting detonated.

So, yes, there is something to do, but again that's being vigilant. That's your real first step. But let's get back to your question, which was about weapons other than guns.

Let's look back at a real example, Columbine again. They had two propane bombs. If you're not aware of the details, they put propane bombs away from the school that they detonated as a ruse for police, to have them dispatched to the wrong places, then they brought two more into the school building. Their plan was to kill hundreds of students in the cafeteria with the bombs and then shoot students who tried to escape the building in the aftermath. When the bombs failed to have the intended effect, they went inside and began shooting people.

This was a situation where something—propane tanks with timers—was odd, something was out of place. People saw those things and did nothing, and that's still the way we operate today as a culture. We see it, and we say nothing. We do nothing.

Q. There are probably a lot of reasons for that, but I think the main one is that we don't want to look foolish, or, God forbid, we don't want to look like we're prejudiced.

I remember when I was maybe 12 or 13, I was walking through my neighborhood after dark one night. It wasn't late, but it was dark. And it was perfectly safe for the kids to do that, going to the store, going back and forth to each other's homes. I was on my way home, and as I passed a house that was on a corner, I saw a guy in the backyard, and it looked to me like he was standing just outside of where the light from the window was falling. I didn't know the people who lived in that house, and it looked suspicious to me. I ran home and called the police. I told them I thought there was a prowler or peeping Tom at that address.

A little while later, a police officer came to my house to let me know what happened. He told me that he approached the house from one direction, another unit came from another direction, and a K-9 unit came from a third direction (remember, this was a corner house that could have been approached from four different directions), they converged on the guy in the backyard all at the same time—and it turned out that he lived there.

I was so embarrassed, and I started to apologize, but the officer wouldn't let me. He told me that I had done the right thing, that the police would rather be called out on lots of these types of calls that turn out to be nothing than to have people not call when they see something that doesn't look right, and something bad happens because nobody called. And this was back in the 1960s, so police have been telling people this for a long time.

Then my mother came home to see the police car in the driveway. She had a few minutes of panic before she could get in the house and realize that everything was fine.

A. And you lived to laugh about it. Now, let's look at what you did.

You saw a threat. Remember, I told you to feel free to stare that person down, so he knows you see him, and you know something is going on. Had you done that, he might have come after you, but he also might have stopped what he was doing. He would have been interrupted. He also may have said, "Oh, I'm just here working in my yard," and explained it. But he didn't do that, so what did you do? You put distance between yourself and a threat. You took the distance you already had and you ran away, you magnified it. You got out of danger and then you notified help.

Yes, you did what was right. You did exactly what we're talking about here. And if that guy that you saw in the dark had a gun and was there to kill every neighbor he could kill—that's pretty extreme—but if that had been the case, you just followed the principles we're laying out here. At age 12, it was still instinctive in you. We work it out of ourselves over time. We worry about offending someone, we worry about looking foolish, so we don't take the right action and we may end up in danger.

Q. Children are far more questioning. They stare openly at people who don't seem right or who look different. They ask questions about people and things they don't understand, and we shush them.

A. Right. We have trained ourselves not to speak up.

Q. *Okay, back to the issue of weapons other than firearms.*

A. Yes, back to explosives. First of all, let's talk Hollywood. Do you cut the red wire or the blue wire?

Q. *I don't know.*

A. Why is anyone going to use a standard for wire color? That's insane! There might be white wires, there might be bare wires, there might be taped wires, who cares?

Now, Hollywood—and this is interesting because our society has adopted another structure: We don't talk about weapons. We have killed the dialogue to the point that we've endangered ourselves. Just as we spoke about guns earlier, let's have that ugly talk about bombs.

If someone has brought a bomb to kill people, there is no elaborate timer. There is no collapsible circuit. There is nothing fancy about it. You have a bomb brought into a situation to help kill people.

The way an explosive works is that something creates an ignition. You've heard of blasting caps. A blasting cap is typically a little tiny silver cylinder, a little thicker than a pencil, with two wires coming out of it. Cut either of those wires and the danger is gone. It can't detonate.

The blasting cap is put inside of a higher-order explosive—the propane tank, the gasoline tank, the gasoline can. So when the wire is ignited and detonates the blasting cap, it detonates the other larger explosive charge. In the case of things like gasoline and propane, you can also use a heated coil and generate heat to the point that it causes an explosion.

The bottom line is there will typically be two wires that are coming into what is called a propellant or explosive charge—

the gas, liquid or solid that holds the explosive charge. They are somehow turned on, activated by a cell phone ring, or activated by a timer or something like that. If you can detach the wires, it's over.

Now, people will tell you there are blasting caps that will go off with millivolts, and that I am giving you dangerous advice. All I'm going to tell you is that those types are few and far between, and someone wanting to kill you won't be carrying one that is at risk of going off in his car or pocket. Because in general, you're not going to find somebody who's picking up a blasting cap that is that dangerous to use in such an uncontrolled environment as an active shooter.

So the bottom line is: You will have a power source connected two wires that are leading into something. Get rid of the two wires, cut them, pull them apart, whatever you need to do. If they're using C-4 or C-6—which looks like putty or clay—again the blasting cap goes straight into it. Detach the wires.

Once you understand this, watch another movie with a bomb. I find them amusing. The bomb technician can stare right at the two wires that are the actual detonator for the explosion and then start to figure out how to disarm the timer. I've detonated C-4 with blasting caps. If you want to make the situation safe, you simply pull the blasting caps out of the C-4 and move them away from the plastic explosive. Yet we see movie after movie where the hero can't figure out what wire to cut or how to stop that blasting cap from going off. Without a dialogue and education, we again find ourselves helpless, convinced that our life hangs in the balance of whether we remembered which color wire we should cut.

Q. So what you're saying is that if you are in a situation and you see something suspicious, and you see wires, pull them out. Or should you call the authorities?

A. Just break the wires in half somehow, get rid of them, because that is your ignition source. Now, what I'm saying to you is this: You can call the authorities. You don't know what will activate the device. If it's on a cell phone, you don't know when the call is being made. You don't know if it's on a timer. So you can call the police.

Q. And it may explode before they get there.

A. It could explode before they get inside the building. They may be there, but they may not be able to enter the building, and it will explode.

Now, again, distance is my friend. If I can get away, I'm doing better. But if I have to protect others in the room, I want to get those wires ripped apart. If you see a wire, cut it. Bite it with your teeth, whatever you need to do. Get it apart. Do not let that circuit exist. There is a loop of electricity going through and it's coming through the wires. There's one coming in and one returning. Cut either one and they're done, cut them both and then you can separate the items. And now the detonator doesn't work anymore. The bomb is disabled.

Now, if you can't do it—say, because they decided to encase it in something. Maybe they put it inside of some kind of steel vault. You're pretty sure there's a bomb, but it's inside a backpack and you're afraid if you open the backpack there's a wire that's going set off the thing, okay? So now you're in a situation where you can't cut the wires. But you're still stuck with the bomb, you can't leave the room, what do you do?

In the case of a gun, you want to get behind as much mass as you can to prevent the bullets from hitting you. The problem with a blast is it's going to spray force and shrapnel in a very broad area at all kinds of velocities and in every imaginable direction. Your best bet with a blast is to encase the explosive. If you can find steel, all the better.

What you are actually able to do is to direct the force of the blast. When the blast comes out, it will reflect off a surface within a small proximity to it and be redirected in another direction. Can you move the bomb against a wall? Can you move it into a closet? Are there a whole bunch of big thick wooden tables that you can just pile up around it that can absorb all that shrapnel and take that impact? You'll have tables flying, there are people who're going to be hurt, but chances are nobody is getting killed.

In the gun situation, you want the insulation around you; in a bomb situation, you want the insulation around the device. A small air gap doesn't matter. You don't have to be right up against it, but pay attention if you decide you're going to use some steel door or something like that because you're forcing that bomb blast to go the other direction. Think about what's in that path. You're not going to feel real good if the other direction was a room full of kids. So do be careful where you refocus that energy. You want to survive, but you don't want to kill anybody else either. You've got to think it through.

Now, again, what are the principles here? Distance is your friend, get away. If you can't get away, if you're trapped with this thing, disable it. Oppose it and disable it. If you can't disable it and you can't control it, it's going to go off. Can you relocate it to a safe place and get away? Can you lock it in a closet inside the room you are in and get to the far end? Can you barricade that closet or can you cover it with every couch cushion, sofa piece and chair in the room and then lock the door behind it and get as far from it as you can?

All of these are ways to thwart it. Once again, just like in the gun incident, it's a hierarchy, it's just that the thought process is different. With the gun, you want to take cover because it's the safer option than engaging to defeat the gun, to get the gun under your control or out of his control. In the bomb situation, you want to encase the bomb if you can do it. If you can't do all those other things and disable it, move it, something like that, you want to cover it as much as you can, to disable it as best you can. It is going to go off in that scenario.

But now once again, having gone through all that, now that you've seen the steps, now step back again and let's get back into the mind of the assailant. He's coming in to kill. He's researched an area where he thinks he can do it without being opposed. Odds are good he's not worried about setting up trip wires and doing special fancy things to his timer on the bomb. He knows he's got maybe 20 minutes, 30 minutes before he's got everybody done. He doesn't expect anybody to come back and oppose him. He's not going to elaborately prepare the bomb.

The bomb oddity comes at the Boston Marathon where they sought to kill people in the open. Now, a bomb is an explosion. An explosion goes in all directions. From a bomber's perspective, the Boston Marathon was not a good place to do it, because you were in the open. Yes, there were a lot of people and it was high visibility. The visibility and media coverage were their intention. What would the same thing have done, the same exact detonator have done in an elevator? In a waiting room? In any other small, crowded place? The casualty level would have been much higher than it was at the Boston Marathon—assuming the same number of people were nearby.

But because their goal was high visibility at a popular public event, the bombers may have put in some extra precautions to prevent someone from tampering with the bomb before they could detonate it. So if you find yourself in a similar situation, what are your opportunities to get away from it?

If you saw something that looks out of place, you report it and then get out of the way, or you get out of the way and then report it. Either way, it's easy to escape it. It's easy to notice it. It's easy it to report it. That's where the failure at the Boston Marathon was.

This is the problem most people who don't know much about explosives are going to have. In their heads, the explosive is the stuff they saw in the movie *Speed*. It is this complicated thing hanging somewhere. There is a bus that's going to blow up if it goes below 50 miles per hour.

That's rubbish. A bomb is a gas can with a heater wire in it. And the bomber has a power supply that, when the cell phone he connects to it activates, trips a relay that lets a lot of power go in from a battery and that sets the bomb off. Take out the battery, cut the wire, it's gone. There is no bus; there is no elevator. There is no colored wire. And even the C-4 in the elevator in that movie—cut the detonator, cut the wires to the blasting cap or pull the blasting caps out of the explosives. The bomb can't do a thing.

Q. So that's what to do if you see something suspicious that turns out to be a bomb.

A. Again, distance is your friend. But if you have to be there with it, disable it. It's not that hard. It's not movie stuff.

Q. *Beyond guns, bombs, and even knives, we're seeing an increase in people using things as weapons that were not intended to be weapons. What comes immediately to mind is using vehicles to run people down in crowded areas. Is there any way to protect yourself against that type of attack?*

A. There are videos online showing the Times Square vehicle attack of May 18, 2017. They're difficult to watch, but they show a true example of a vehicle attack. A friend of mine in law enforcement shared video from several surveillance cameras that showed the event from multiple angles. Here's what happened:

The driver passes on one side of the road, traveling in traffic like any other vehicle. He makes a casual left turn but turns that action into a U-turn which he uses to accelerate and move onto the sidewalk, running over many pedestrians. He continues to drive for blocks until crashing onto a barrier and attempting to run away from the scene. Most news articles focus on the assailant, but our focus here is the victims and potential victims.

At the moment of the U-turn, the only thing odd is that the vehicle is accelerating, which is not entirely uncommon. The people on the wide NYC sidewalk that were first struck truly had no notice, no triggers, and no options. I'm sorry to use the term helpless, but they were exactly that. The people taken down in the first three seconds of the event truly had no options.

The people of New York City are no strangers to violence and that showed in their response. They became alert. People began to run for cover as the vehicle approached. They did not ignore the oncoming threat, but instead looked over their shoulders and prepared for it. They moved to cover and exited the path of the vehicle in numbers. Unfortunately, some did trip or fall and were struck.

The vehicle targeted hundreds of people. In the end, only one died and twenty were injured because of what the New Yorkers did: They *paid attention, prepared, and took action*. This pattern repeated near the World Trade Center grounds in October 2017 when the driver of a rented pickup truck attempted to run over hundreds of bikers and pedestrians. He killed eight and injured eleven, but he was trying to do more.

The New York City residents apply the principles of this book and live through these events as a result. Pay attention. Know what to do. Take action.

I wonder if other cities would have handled the situation as well. If people live in a culture of isolation or believe "I hear screaming but that's none of my business," then I fear that the results would be far worse. New Yorkers know better and survive.

When I learned to drive in an area prone to snow, I was taught to always keep in mind where to direct the car if I needed to avoid an accident, if someone stopped suddenly, or if some other unexpected situation occurred. The lesson was to always have a plan B. The other lane? Well, not if it had oncoming traffic. The side of the road? Not if it was a cliff. But always think about where to direct the car in the event of a problem.

New Yorkers did the same thing as pedestrians when they were attacked by a vehicle—they immediately recognized danger and engaged their plan B. It's a thought process that can save lives, whether for a casual driver or a potential victim of vehicular manslaughter or homicide.

CHAPTER ELEVEN

How Do You Handle a Hostage Situation When You're the Hostage?

Question: What should you do if you are taken hostage? I know you told me when we were preparing for this conversation that doesn't happen often, but people see it in on television and in the movies, so let's talk about it.

Answer: Actually, Mateen did it at the Pulse in Orlando. Mateen came in with a plan. The plan was to have a fish-in-a-barrel situation. He was just going to shoot and mow them all down. He ran out of targets and he didn't know what he was doing anymore.

He took hostages at times, he shot at piles of dead, maybe for movement or maybe not, and he started going into weird rooms. His whole method of operation fell apart after his fish-in-a-barrel scenario wasn't working anymore. So taking hostages is a reality in some cases but it's going to be a late measure. It's going to be towards the end.

Now, this is difficult to explain in a book. It's much easier to demonstrate. But let's give it a try.

You're now a hostage—and we're talking about a hostage in the physical possession of the assailant. You know about the interruption of the OODA loop. You are right there up close and personal. Anything you do disrupts his actions. Go into an act from the *Three Stooges*, flick his ear, give him a wedgie with his underwear, yank on his belt, yank off his belt, hit his gun while he's shooting. You are the disruption. Don't feel helpless, feel powerful.

Now, at some point, as soon as you can, you want to get away. Think about ways to defeat the weapon. Grab it and take it from him if it's a long gun, jam your finger behind the trigger if you have to. Once your finger is behind that trigger and ideally bent over and holding the gun, that gun is yours, not his. He can't shoot you.

If you can picture this: He has the gun and he has his finger on the trigger, and your finger is going the other way behind the trigger and wrapped around the trigger cage—most handguns have a trigger cage. If that's the case, you now own the weapon. When you pull it, it will come out of his hands. When he pulls, your hand is in the way. When he tries to squeeze the trigger with all his might, your finger will break. But it will heal, and now that gun is your gun. Run. Don't hold that weapon up, just run. You just got your way to escape.

If it's a rifle, you may have burned your hands on the barrel, but it's yours. Club the crap out of that man. Knock him out and beat him senseless. You have every reason to. Everybody else's life is at stake too. Get the gun away from him, beat him with it if you can, and then run. Don't worry about hurting him—remember, he wanted to kill you.

Here's another tactic. If you ever take a basic self-defense class, you may learn this. If the man has his arm around you and his palm in front of you, dead center of the palm is a very sensitive nerve, so make yourself a very large knuckle with your largest finger and jam it straight into the center of his hand, and that hand will break loose.

If he is holding you and standing behind you, the exact same rule fits for the top center of the foot. Stomp on it and it will hurt. Or if you want to—and you do!—try to cripple him for life. With all of your might, kick him straight into the kneecap with the back of your heel and you will shatter his kneecap and he will never walk again. Remember, this is someone who wants to kill you and everyone dear to you.

Warning: The following paragraph is extremely graphic.

You have other interesting options. If you can face him, take your finger and press into the eye at the point nearest the nose. Keep pressing until you cannot press anymore. You will remove his eye. That will finish his rampage. If you have a way to blind him, then do so—90 percent of his information just got denied and he is frozen. Slam the flat of your hand into his nose straight-on and break his nose. You may not stop him, but the pain will be an effective stop to his aim and shoot activities. This is before we consider other things like pulling hair, kidney punches and the like. If you are his hostage, and you are in close, then do not think yourself powerless. You are now the most powerful person in that room, and you can hurt him like no other. You can also control the aim of his gun and, while terribly risky, can fire it at his own extremities. Distance makes you safer. Being pressed against the assailant makes you more powerful. It is the places in between that hold the greatest danger.

Q. *So don't worry about the pain you might be inflicting on him.*

A. This is life and death. He is willing to take your life, and you are applying equal force. Do what you need to do to survive. When you can, run. But all of those options are available to you. He will know some of them that he will avoid, but you will be able to do some of them. He can't protect himself from all of them, so be ready to go.

CHAPTER TWELVE

Does the Motive of the Shooter Matter?

Question: *Let's talk about the difference between the active shooter who is on a mission to do mass murder with the goal of getting a body count as high as possible and a shooter who is after one or just a few specific targets, such as a domestic violence situation where the shooter is trying to kill a spouse or lover, or a workplace violence situation where the shooter wants to kill a manager or certain coworkers. What's the difference in how you deal with those situations?*

Answer: Overall, there's no difference except that we've focused on a specific setting.

I said earlier to pay attention to the person. If they are someone you work with, you're going to see the changes over time. But the distinction here is not the event. The distinction here is your control of the setting.

In a workplace environment, you should have a way to vet those coming in regularly. You should be escorting those who are not regularly in your facility. Always have somebody with them. It limits their ability to do anything.

If you're in an office of five people; the five of you are looking out for each other. Who's the sixth person coming in? Somebody get on top of them.

Are they going to draw that weapon and shoot their spouse when somebody is right next to them who could do who-knows-what to them? What if they have to stop and sign in, but they weren't able to balance all the stuff they are carrying to do that? Any weaponry may become exposed before they reach the intended target or targets. You disrupted their plan since you had a solid vetting practice in place.

So the difference isn't in how you handle a situation that went really bad, the difference is that you can keep the situation from going really bad.

The Pulse, the movie theater, the restaurant—they can't vet everybody coming in. That's an impossible scenario. But the typical office building, yes, you can. Maybe you want to do background checks. If you have somebody who starts to look a little hokey, you may want to do it or may want to say, "Hey, you know, the company has a program for people under stress, we see you're under stress, we'd like to help." And three weeks before he goes crazy and starts shooting people, you've got him sitting in with a therapist.

Or let's go another route. In most states, the law is that if you prove that someone is a danger to himself or others, it's time to call the authorities. So when Jim down the hall on day one says, "That evil woman left me." On day two, he's upset because she left him for Bob, her supervisor, and on day three, he says, "I could just kill him," there is a definite clue there of what you should doing.

Q. Along with this, you need to provide a vehicle for your employees to speak up, to get help, if they are either in a potentially dangerous domestic situation or if they see behavior changes in someone else.

A. In large companies, you have a human resources department, employee assistance programs and other resources for people to use. But let's say you're in a company of five. In a company that small, you know each other well. So when Jill's husband shows up for the first time after she's been working there for several years, or even several weeks, and indicates a tone of hostility, don't ignore it. It's time to say, "Hey, we're coworkers, we're friends, we're concerned." And tell her husband too: "We see you two are under a lot of stress, what can we do to help?"

Remember, for him to kill he has to demonize. Here you are before he's hit that point, saying, "How do we help?"

If you miss your opportunity and you start to hear him say "I can't wait to kill that bastard" or some kind of evil words like that, it's time to call the police and bring this under the attention of professionals. The police will have him evaluated. And guess what? If you're wrong, he's going to be mad at you—but if nothing was wrong, he has that opportunity and you can always apologize.

But if something was wrong...

Q. And you didn't do anything...

A. People could die.

Now, if I may add one other thing. When we talked about an office setting, we also discussed the explosives, the strange objects. In an office setting, you have more of a static environment than anywhere else. When something appears that doesn't look right, do not ignore it. If your office is under some sort of threat, let it be known to the police, react to it, take it seriously. Again, there's a million threats—domestic violence, workplace violence, even angry customers or vendors. If you're in an office that you know is likely to be attacked, this may sound weird, but one of the greatest things you can have is a powerful fountain.

Q. A drinking fountain?

A. No, a decorative fountain. If you have a large and powerful water fountain that is pressurizing water and an explosive charge goes through it, the force will deflect into a new direction, generally up. Whatever is coming through it, it will cool it down and it will dissipate its energy. So if for some reason you believe that your facility will at some point be targeted, fountains are your friends. And I'm not telling you to install a fountain on every wall of your office building, that's not practical. But if you're worried about something and it's a small area, and you don't want to be putting up steel bars, think about something that's pumping a lot of water off to the side. And ironically a fountain has a soothing effect on the people coming up to it. Fountains are known to calm people. So it adds that value too.

Q. Is there any reason for us to spend time talking about the difference between a shooter who is mentally ill versus one who is a radicalized terrorist on a mission to do what he be-

lieves is right? I'm thinking of the difference between the Sandy Hook shooter and the Boston Marathon bombers.

A. We've kind of already touched on this. If you wish to do harm to yourself or others, you are by definition mentally ill. Your motivation is secondary to that; you are mentally ill. Both types of shooters are mentally ill because they are willing to kill others.

Now, granted, it's a dogmatic approach describing you if you're a radical Islamic terrorist, but the bottom line is you have turned people into targets. They're no longer human beings. You cannot recognize the good in them, you cannot recognize the unity you have with them. They are simply objects to be destroyed to make a point. And that's in either case, that's a mental illness issue.

From the victim's perspective, there's really no difference. What's important to remember is that no matter what the motivation, once they are in a mode where you've seen them shoot people, they are shooting, they are killing people, even if it's someone you know, it's not the time to go up and say, "It's really good to see you, I've missed you, how have you been?"

There is no reasoning anymore. The time for that has passed. Any opportunity you had to intervene is gone, now your job is to survive. Do not try and rationalize. Do not try to reason. There is no reason left. They've gotten rid of it. Just do what you have to do to survive.

CHAPTER THIRTEEN

Do You Have Additional Tips for Safety in Public Places?

Question: We've talked some about ways to stay safe when you're in public places—know where the exits are, pay attention to the people around you. What else do you want to say about that?

Answer: The bottom line remains that distance is your friend.

If you're going to a public event, choose the area where you're going to sit or be. That's a difficult one. You have to know the exit you can get out of, but on the other hand, you may be face-to-face with the guy who just came in that same exit you were counting on. I can't tell you how to do that, do "what's important now" and choose your seat.

If you feel that you're in danger, get away from that danger. At least know your exits. The middle seat of a movie theater—it's going to take you a long time to get to the end of that row and get out, which makes you a target. Then again, from the middle seat, you have your choice of which exit to use, which is a choice you won't have if you're sitting right next to one. So I can't tell you that there's one specific answer. Do what's best for the situation.

If you ever spend time in the Southwest, you will notice one of the "codes of the West" still being followed to this day. Whenever a couple comes into a restaurant or bar and sits down, they have assigned seats. Think about that a moment—think about Western movies and what you've seen. The male sits facing the door. He is the one responsible for the protection of the couple or the family. By facing the door, he is positioned to take the first action if a threat enters. It's not something that's discussed, it's just done. The only way you will even know it's happening is by noticing the trend or having a close friend from the West tell you how awkward it is to see you with your back toward the door if you're male. So learn from the code of the West—if you dine alone, face the door. You just got a few more seconds to get ahead of the situation.

Q. What about choosing where to park your car?

A. Parking questions are real interesting ones, you know. Again, if you're going to worry about where you're parking, you already feel you're in danger. That's the reality. So odds are you're not going to go through that thought process when you're parking. But let's suppose for some reason you do. You've heard something might happen in your area and you're really freaked out. Northern Virginia once had a Halloween threat against a shopping mall. They were threatening to gas people in a mall. So let's walk that model, through a parking lot.

So where would you park? Obviously, you're going to want to park where you can get out quickly, but you also want to be able to reach the cover of your car quickly.

But now think of a shopping mall. It's designed to bring people in and park their cars. And the people will have to be exiting through the very same exits that are the entrances for the emergency services vehicles. It will be a mess. You'll be trapped in a line. So you know what? Quit worrying about the curbs, just drive over them. Quit worrying about your car. Try not to hurt anybody else and get out of there as fast as you can. Even the fire trucks and police cars will be ignoring the curbs because they have to get in. When you need to get out, think outside the box and do what you have to do to get to a safe place.

CHAPTER FOURTEEN

What Specific Advice do you have for Protecting Houses of Worship from an Attack?

Q. Perhaps one of the most vulnerable places in our lives is a church setting. We sit and worship, often close our eyes, and place our children in adjoining buildings. What can we do to ensure our safety in a house of worship?

A. Before I answer that, I think that every church-going reader should know that there are numerous high-quality resources on the internet addressing church security. Many of them are quite brilliant. If you read this text, go beyond it and research the strategies and tactics that best fit your particular house of worship.

Remember that just about every church building is different. The number of doors, windows, distance to the classrooms, size of the congregation, number of floors, presence of a balcony will all change the approach to safety and security to some degree. Reviewing the thoughts of different experts will far better inform you than what I can tell you myself.

Much of the advice I have for churches can be applied to other types of facilities with no or just a small amount of modification.

With that said, I will lay a foundation. You should build on it to cover the distinctions of your own house of worship. Also consider your local resources—many towns and counties will offer a free security consultation to their local churches.

The first step is to picture your church in your mind. Get down to the details. Answer these questions:

- Where are the doors and windows?
- Where are the bushes and shrubs?
- Where can someone enter without detection?
- Are there any blind spots where either a member of the congregation could disappear from view or an assailant could readily hide?
- Does everything work?
- Do the locks work?
- Do the doors seal?
- Is there a practice to ensure that the doors, windows, and locks continue to function?
- Is there anything showing that your church is not in good repair, such as lingering graffiti, broken windows, or other neglect that would tell someone that they can likely target your church effectively?
- Do the light bulbs all work?

- Do you have a good security system—ideally one that includes motion detectors?

Once you have positive answers to all those concerns, you can move on to more specific items. Let's assume that you have all the issues we just listed covered. You still want to be sure that people can escape rapidly if they need to do so. Panic bars, or crash bars, are a great idea for the doors in any place where people will gather. Consider getting ones with alarms for doors you don't normally want to use, such as emergency only exits.

Depending on your floorplan, you may want to consider making sure that some sort of visibility exists between rooms. This could necessitate adding viewing windows. Those little panes of glass can help someone in another room recognize a problem and get assistance, or help first responders gain a tactical advantage without breaching a door.

Also, be aware that many people are convinced that technology offers immediate security solutions. We can protect our homes with cameras, as our main concern is a break-in when we are away, and the camera lets us find the villain and regain our property. When we fear for the safety of lives, many people try to reapply that logic and think a camera is a solution. It isn't.

If a person or congregation is vulnerable, then adding a camera gives us an opportunity to see who is coming—but the vulnerability remains. A motion detector can sound an alarm telling us to look at the monitor, but we are still no safer. A metal detector can tell us if the person is armed, but we are still no safer and are more likely to be harmed when that detector goes off. Knowledge is power after the fact.

The only way to protect people against a threat is with a response. It can be as basic as a locking door—provided that the door will survive an attempt at penetration (and that there is no nearby vulnerable window)—or it can be people ready to engage. A camera protects no one—it just helps figure out who did the deed after the deed was done. A response is needed.

Now that we've addressed the condition, role, and importance of the doors, windows, security systems, and locks, it's time to think more deeply. You need to *be the people*.

Q. What do you mean by that?

A. Think of your property from the perspective of all the people who might be there, from your congregation to an attacker. Let's list them:

1. **An assailant.** This would be someone who wants to kill or take hostage as many as possible. Think about your church through his eyes. Where will he park? Where will he enter? Where will he move? Consider that he may pre-survey the property, even attending some church events to learn the lay of the land. Do *not* assume that you have any advantage for things about the property that he doesn't know. Be him. Which door will he kick down? What if he comes during a church event when the doors are open? And now the hardest question for any church: How will you oppose him?

2. **An arsonist.** This would be someone who wants to destroy the church, possibly including a high number of victims. Think about it through his

eyes. Where will he strike? What can you do to make him not want to choose that point or to choose a target other than your church?

3. **A villain.** This is someone who wants to steal from the church or someone at the church. What will make him think there is something of value? What will draw him to your church? How do you make him see your church as less of a target?

4. **A child.** This is a youngster who is away from his mom and dad in one of your educational facilities, with other children and one or two instructors. This child is one of your most vulnerable people. How are you protecting that child and giving that child the potential to escape to safety? Have you considered the risks? What training have you decided to provide?

5. **A handicapped person.** This is someone who is unable to have normal freedom of movement—another of your most vulnerable. How do you ensure that person's safety in whatever setting they normally would be found? Remember, we are talking about the worst of the worst—possible active shooters, kidnappers, bombers, and arsonists. Can you get the handicapped of your congregation to safety?

6. **An elderly person.** Just as with handicapped people, the elderly are among your most vulnerable people. If the rest of the congregation is racing out the door, how would an elderly person constrained by a walker or cane manage to escape to safety?

7. **People outside the main congregational gathering.** These are the people who are engaged in some function in small numbers, such as the preacher, choir, band, music director, lighting manager, school teacher, or anyone else that is not part of a mass group at any time. Their individual vulnerabilities will be different from those of the masses.
8. **The primary centers of mass.** This is the congregation gathered for worship or another reason, the classes, the various staff members, or whatever large gatherings of people you have that should be considered as a group.
9. **Vehicle operators.** Particularly in suburban and rural areas, but even in cities, people will come and go by vehicle and also park their vehicles. Those vehicles also have safety and security issues, as does the parking lot and points of entry and exit from the facility.

Your church may have others, like groundskeepers or a sexton, or some other function that adds to this list. Make the list your own. The goal here is to be thorough and thus be prepared. It's not to be paranoid nor fearful. You are protecting—not frightening—with these processes.

Before I move on, let's also mention a few circumstances that churches frequently experience that other types of facilities may not.

Some churches may be adjacent to high crime areas or even homeless camps and suffer break-ins of the main facility or outbuildings or have people sleep in their driveways from time to time, which creates vehicular hazards. Some may be of a special cultural significance that offends other neighboring cultures and are targets for vandalism. Some may be seen as the local treasure trove because they are more ornate than anything else in the area and be a target for those needing money. Some may be adjacent to major roads with quick ingress/egress options, thus encouraging thefts from vehicles during church activities. Some may exist in bad neighborhoods and need security to escort people to and from the outer parking areas.

Your church is unique, and you need to consider the full spectrum of risks as you make your assessments.

Q. *So when you think about protecting your church from an attacker, you need to do a general security review.*

A. Yes. The principles of security overlap. If you're spending the effort to protect your church from a mass killing, then think through the rest. Every vulnerability you address will protect you from theft and vandalism as well.

Also understand that each church will handle this situation differently, and Hollywood has impacted the thoughts of many. If a large group works on security, then expect every movie-inspired form of fear to come forward, no matter how valid or invalid. In the movies, people are accurately killed from handguns being fired in passing vehicles traveling at high speed. In reality, a shooter is lucky to hit the building with a shot. In the movies, cars blow up immediately when a gas tank is near the point of a bullet's penetration. The odds of that happening are minuscule. In the movies, every shooter hits someone with every shot. In reality, even trained police officers have a hit rate during times of crisis of less than 20 percent. In the movies, a pocket-sized bomb destroys a building. I've worked with explosives and never seen something that small do that much damage. Be ready to deal with the unreal, and research it or get a professional to help you educate your people. Their fears are real, but the basis of those fears may be fictional.

Q. That's a good point—and another good reason to do this.

A. Now let's talk about what to do when an attack begins. We'll cover all three situations we've been discussing: a shooter, a bomb, and a vehicular attack. I'll cover them in reverse order since the complexities increase as we move to an active shooter event.

Q. So the first one is a vehicular attack.

A. I've had the displeasure of being inside a movie theater when a car hit the back wall. The car only hit the wall at about 20 mph, but the impact caused a sudden bang, the curtains hanging on the wall moved outwards against the audience, and the block wall damaged. Yes, many people screamed and were shaken up, but no one was killed or even injured. This was around 1979 before terrorism was a major concern in the U.S. It was not an attack, it was an accident.

But what would have happened if the small car had instead been a large truck? If it were moving at 90 mph instead of 20 mph?

For your church, think in terms of opportunity to commit a vehicular attack. Can the attacker achieve a high velocity and strike your people or your walls? You'll find that there are only a few areas where most churches can say yes to that question, and those are the areas on which you should focus.

These are the areas able to be struck by a vehicle that came off a high-speed road and never needed to slow down before impacting the church. These are the areas with a good quarter-mile or more of uninterrupted, straight terrain allowing a vehicle to build up speed before it hits.

You can move your people away from the vulnerable parts of the structure. For example, you can have preferred seating away from the wall most likely to be struck. You can plant trees or bushes to remove the path for the driver to accelerate, add concrete monuments to that path, or remove straight line roads in favor of tree-lined pathways.

Take away the ability for a vehicle to achieve speed at impact and you take away much of the risk. Remember, too, that convenience stores are sometimes robbed by racing a truck into a pair of glass doors, breaking their frames. The open parking lots give enough room to achieve the velocity and impact needed to execute the theft. So don't think about just a full parking lot where cars could restrict the ability to achieve velocity—think about your parking lot being empty overnight or when only a few people are there, and whether it allows someone to build up speed and breach the facility.

Q. Let's go to the second scenario, a bomb.

A. Bombs get more complicated to address. Is the bomb inside or outside? Is it in a fixed or mobile position? How is it shaped? Each of these answers changes the situation significantly.

When we talked about what weapons attackers use, we talked about explosions. That's worth repeating and expanding.

We all know that a bomb is a device that explodes, so let's discuss an explosion again. An explosion is a *sudden* equalization of pressure. Take your two index fingers and tap them together. Do you hear that faint sound? What you hear is the sound of skin impacting skin. Now clap. Do you hear that loud pop? Why is that sound so different from the sound of skin impacting skin?

Because a clap is an explosion. You are trapping air inside your palms and then compressing it. When it suddenly equalizes with the outside pressure, it releases a blast called an explosion. The seal of your skin around the air is ruptured, allowing the trapped air to release. The sound you hear is the same thing, on a smaller scale, as a blast wave or pressure wave. All sound carries as a compression wave—a force of pressure carried through the molecules of the air that makes your eardrum vibrate. The same can be said of popping bubble wrap, popping a balloon, or even a car backfire. Suddenly pressure has equalized. We have experienced an explosion, no matter how trivial.

Now let's think about a bomb. A bomb is typically a container holding something that will build pressure, meaning that it will ignite. The Columbine attackers detonated propane bombs. Television regularly shows us gasoline bombs, and there is speculation that the Las Vegas shooter tried to detonate fuel tanks at nearby McCarran airport. We also see images of TNT, DNT, C-4, and other high explosive compounds being detonated. In each case, a sudden amount of pressure builds, breaks open a seal, and releases its payload of heat, fuel, and pressure.

Why do you need to know this information? Because it tells you how to predict the blast pattern of a bomb.

What is the most likely point where the pressure will vent? That is the place where the blast will be strongest. If you think about a metal pipe bomb, then the seams of the caps where they connect to the shaft are that point. If you think about a plastic pipe bomb, then the blast will be more uniform than the metal one, but the intersection of the shaft and cap will again be the most likely. The propane bombs at Columbine would have been most lethal at the point where the detonator pierced the casing. That point of the largest blast volume tells you where the bulk of the blast is heading. It also tells you what to expect when the detonation occurs.

If the bomb is placed outside your church, you want to get people to safety. This can be a rapid exit from the area, or it can be a rapid entry to a more protected area.

Triggers may be timers, cell phones, buzzers, beepers, weight detectors, motion detectors, or anything else that can decide when to detonate the bomb, so you can never be certain how much time you have between the current moment and the moment of detonation. Distance and protection are your best goals.

Similarly, there is great risk for anyone on the other side of a wall with a bomb targeting it. They also need to focus on distance and protection.

If you believe an outdoor bomb attack is a risk at your church, then consider what I just said. How do you ensure people get to cover? Can you create some sort of large structure to isolate the blast, the people, or both? If you have a small area of your outer wall that is a likely risk, then consider installing a fountain to block that wall. Fountains significantly disrupt every effect of a bomb and will reduce its impact.

Q. What about a bomb inside?

A. The indoor bomb is more problematic. We have a box scenario—limited egress and people trapped inside a container. Their evacuation route could also be set to trigger a detonation. What can a layperson do in such an event?

The first and most important thing to do is to pay attention to your surroundings. That big cardboard box in the corner that wasn't there last week could be something nefarious. Draw attention to it—ask about it. The more time you have to address the existence of an explosive, the better.

If you believe there is a threat, then get away as fast as possible. If the doors are all locked, then cover the threat in the heaviest materials that you can find and get yourself to whatever cover you have left. By trapping the blast inside a framework of heavy objects, the blast effect reduces—but also throws heavy objects.

I don't want to tell you to diffuse the bomb, but if you have the knowledge and your life is on the line, that may not be a bad idea—but get others heading to protective covering first. Use the water balloon concept we talked about earlier. If you picture that bomb as a huge water balloon, where can you go where you won't get wet when it goes off? That spot is typically going to keep you safe. Remember to plug your ears, too. You will likely suffer hearing loss after an explosion in an enclosed area.

Package bombs sent through the mail have been a threat for years and can typically be identified by certain odd features. If you see a package with a partial address, no specific name, major misspellings, an oily residue or powder coming from the sides, and/or a foreign sender's address, then you have a potential threat. Get people away from the threat and notify authorities.

There are millions of forms of potential explosive devices, and each situation is different. When it comes to churches, a structure made of glass will fare far worse in an explosion than one made of block. One with short ceilings will fare far worse than one with tall ceilings. If you don't feel that you can make the right assessment for how to deal with a possible explosive device, contact your local law enforcement and ask for advice before you face the situation in real life.

Now you need to think beyond the bomb itself. Remember when we discussed being the people? Do it again.

You find the bomb—what do you do with the children in the separate building? What evacuation routes do you endorse? If the bomber is nearby ready to dial the cell phone, pager, or radio that will set off the bomb, where is he and can you deny him access to that spot? Can you evacuate without him seeing you? If you have exits to the parking area and also exits to protected rooms, he is more likely outside watching, ready to make an escape, or somewhere inside? Do your best to evacuate everyone away from the doors—once they open, the bomb may go off. Your goal is to save as many lives as possible.

Q. Now let's talk about the scenario that sparked this book: an active shooter.

A. Before we even begin, this discussion will be scrutinized for practicality, morality, and legality issues. Let me address them upfront.

First, practicality. If someone enters your church with a gun, intent on shooting others, please identify *every* possible means to stop him. Don't try to reason with him. If you recall when we talked about demonizing the enemy, you'll remember that he is already beyond reason.

Second, morality. There were no guns in Jesus' day; however, there are references to weapons within the Bible. These can be interpreted many ways, and we're not debating theology here. What's important is that you do not clearly ban nor solicit the presence of weapons in a church.

Third, legality. Guns may be carried into a house of worship in 48 states. Several states require the permission of the house of worship first. If your church hosts a school, then other laws may apply. Learn the laws of your locality. The laws won't protect you from the shooter, but they will determine what options you legally possess to stop one.

There are more than 300 million guns in America. There are 323.1 million Americans. So do the math: 323.1 million Americans possessing over 300 million guns equals how many active shooter events per year?

On average, the answer is 10 to 12 depending on the source you check.

Your odds of experiencing an active shooter event are minimal. According to a 2013 FBI study, houses of worship represented 3.8 percent of those events, with businesses at 45.6 percent and schools at 24.4 percent being the most frequent sites.

In the National Safety Council's 2017 injury facts chart, which shows the most likely causes of injury, heart disease and cancer were the largest, at 1 in 7. Chronic lower respiratory disease was second, at 1 in 28. Assault by firearm was seventh, at 1 in 370, and includes accidents, suicides, and hunting incidents. Self-harm, unintentional poisoning, motor vehicle accidents, and falls were numbers three through six.

There are many other sources that identify your chances of dying by gunfire or a mass shooter, and in every case, the odds are minimal.

I share all of this because many churches choose to do nothing or to use faith as their method of protection. While the statistics are in your favor, the approach isn't practical—nor is it effective if an actual active shooter event emerges.

Active shooter preparation is not pleasant and creates anxiety within a church and among its members. The issue can divide on moral and political lines. I urge you not to let your views on guns and "gun control" get in the way of effectively preparing your congregation or other group to survive an attack. We have to look at the way things are, not at the way we wish them to be. So let's talk about the best way to deal with an active shooter.

There is only one effective way to deal with an armed person intent on shooting others and that's with a gun. Active shooters generally attempt to avoid confrontation with armed persons. There have been events—the Clackamas Mall incident being the best documented—where the active shooter abandoned his goal or committed suicide once facing armed retaliation.

Don't get me wrong—I am actually not advocating simply carrying guns to church. There is a grave danger in that, too. You need a plan.

So to protect yourself from an active shooter, consider first how to identify and handle an active shooter. Some common thoughts church members offer, whether good or bad, are:

1. Do nothing;

2. Pray;
3. Post "gun free zone signs";
4. Establish a group to protect the church;
5. Train a group to protect the church.

So let's go through them. Doing nothing and praying may work because the actual risk is minimal. Mathematically, if churches have 3.8 percent of the active shooter events and if we use the overly broad "death by firearm" category, your odds of dying at church by a firearm are about 1 in 10,000.

In 2012 and 2014, 80 people died each year of mass shooting events. That makes your odds of dying in a mass shooting event 80/323.1 million or 1 in over 4 million. If church is only 3.8% of those, then your odds are 1 in 105 million. I have full respect for any church that chooses to pray or to do nothing—with two caveats.

The danger of posting a gun free zone sign is the first caveat. A shooter wants to be unopposed. If you post a gun free zone sign, then you have just volunteered your congregation for attack. Your goal is to dissuade the attacker—if he wishes to kill random people in numbers, then he will do so. You don't want your church to be the target. The gun free zone sign works against that goal. Posting that sign tells the shooter that this is a place where he can attack and be unopposed. It's a welcome mat to him. Plus, it's a wholly ineffective concept. If you believe that a person who has come to a building with the intent to kill, carrying weapons and ammunition with him, will look at a piece of paper saying "gun free zone" and say, "Aw, shucks—gotta do it somewhere else now," then I really wish I could live in that world with you. No law, no paper, no policy will stop a person intent on killing.

Establishing a group to protect the church is the next caveat. I carry a weapon to church. I know what I would do if threatened. However, I also have one great fear that comes from knowing that there is no group training: What will the rest of the congregation do?

In an unprepared church, no one knows who is or is not armed. No one knows who is or is not trained. Let's suppose twelve people oppose the shooter with their guns. What will the outcome be? Friendly fire deaths are more likely. Chaos and panic are more likely. How will the other eleven react to me? How will I react to them? Will any of us shoot each other, or miss the shooter and accidentally kill a member of the congregation? Leaving it all to chance is a dangerous move.

Further, we discussed the congregation. What about the people in other areas of the church? Do we have an ability to lock down the facility? Can we effectively reunite families after the event? How do we know what is happening across the entire facility—is possible that there is a shooter in the sanctuary, another in the school, and another in the kitchen?

Leaving everything to chance brings about its own risks and dangers. The possibility does exist that the presence of the firearms may cause more harm than good, even if used to protect the church. The active shooter will cause every person present to behave in a new and unexpected way. Movement will be unpredictable. The most dangerous person in the room may not be the active shooter but could become the well-meaning member of the congregation trying to stop him, but from a distance with a backdrop of dozens or hundreds of panicking people. Or it may be the very panicked individual trampling the children and elderly in an attempt to get away.

So the right answer is number five: Train a group to protect the church. That is their role. Period. They do not pass collection plates. They do not participate in the choir. They do not hand out leaflets or food items. They do not assist in communion. They protect the church.

They should be *trained together* and, ideally, armed. Their existence should be known to the church membership through verbal communication, not published information. They should meet periodically to evaluate potential threats and vulnerabilities and be ready to address them. This can include theft, kidnapping, bombs, and other concerns of the church, as the church now has trained personnel working to establish secure surroundings. People who will check for lights, dark areas, hiding spaces, tripping hazards now exist. They will know where to either sit or walk during each church activity. They should never be permitted to become a social club—they cannot simply chat amongst themselves during church gatherings. They must be either positioned or properly mobile to ensure the church is safeguarded.

Q. It seems like this trained group would protect against more than an active shooter.

A. Yes. This trained group reduces your church's vulnerability to the entire spectrum of threats from theft to safety to crime. It is the wisest approach to protect your church from *every* threat.

Q. What about a situation where such a group does not exist but there are people who are carrying weapons?

A. If you are someone who carries a weapon to church to see to the safety of others, please consider your own tactics.

If you see a suspicious person, move close to him. The greater distance from the threat means the greater the chance that you could miss and hit someone or something else if you need to fire your weapon.

Think about your ammunition. Jacketed hollow point (JHP) bullets will impact your target, lose velocity, and begin to tumble. The odds of a second casualty from a through-and-through round are minimized with hollow point bullets. But remember that your adversary is probably shooting something else that will very likely pierce through a thin material or person and remain lethal--perhaps a full metal jacket (FMJ) round.

Consider where you sit. The shooter will likely engage from the main entry or center of the church. Be in the center of the church so that you can immediately respond. Sit on the end of your row or pew so that you can move quickly.

Also, if your church is preparing to train a group to protect the church, reach out to local law enforcement and security-trained members of your congregation and ask for advice. Document the plan so that new members can come on board quickly, and so that church leaders know the plan.

Some key things to consider in planning include the entries and exits, including windows, that may be used; how to lock down portions of the church facility during the event; alarm systems; best paths to achieve a rapid exit; what cover exists in what areas; how people can reach law enforcement; whether alarms or detection systems are needed; what hallways, tunnels, and other paths may add vulnerability or require coverage; how a shooter would escape; who could be taken hostage if a lockdown is not implemented.

Think about your church and its layout. *Be the people*.

Q. *What would you say to a church leader who has read this and decided not to follow your advice?*

A. I would say this: You've decided that my advice on having an armed force is a bad move, not in keeping with your faith or morals, and unacceptable. That's fine, but it doesn't mean that you should dismiss the other elements we discussed. You actually have some non-lethal options. They will not save you, but they may buy you vital seconds during an attack. A trained, prepared, armed response will save almost every life. But here are some tips that will save some lives, and I apologize for repeating them.

Over 90 percent of the information that we receive comes through our eyes. Shining a bright light into someone's eyes causes them to freeze. A sufficiently bright light may temporarily blind them. If you have the option to flood the assailant with bright lights, you will freeze his actions and also make him unable to see past the source of the light. You will get added time to get some people to safety, and may give a light-filled "smoke screen" of invisibility to your congregation. Try it yourself—have someone shine a bright flashlight in your face and see if you can continue to function. You will rapidly learn the tactic.

The reason this works is more than just optics. Every human being takes actions by a four-part sequence called the OODA loop. We've already talked about this, but it's worth repeating. We *observe* what is around us. We *orient* ourselves to the situation. We *decide* on what we will do. We *act*.

If you can disrupt the attacker's OODA loop, you can stop the action from occurring. The flashlight example has a screening and blinding effect, but it also changes the *observe* and *orient* pieces of the shooter's operation. He freezes briefly in order to re-observe and re-orient. If he is temporarily blinded, this process takes longer.

If you have a gathering of people, check how quickly you can point at another person. It will likely take less than a second. Next, do the same thing but have a person throw things—softballs, ping-pong balls, crayons, whatever. See how long it takes. You should find that the time required increased three- to ten-fold. Do it again and change the lighting. Do it again and have someone scream. Anything that disrupts the OODA loop stops the action—at least for a few seconds.

So if your church decides that a security team is the wrong approach, then please at least take the time to teach them to disrupt an attacker's OODA loop. Having 100 people randomly yelling, throwing, changing light levels, etc. will diminish the attacker's abilities for a few seconds each time. It won't save everyone, but it will save some.

CHAPTER FIFTEEN

Can You Teach Children to Survive an Active Shooter Situation?

Question: There's no way to shield children from news reports of massacres. I think that's one of the hardest parts of being a parent today—so much ugly, frightening news. Parents try to teach their kids to be safe, but it's one thing to tell them to always look both ways before crossing the street and altogether something else to talk about what they should do if someone starts shooting.

Answer: Okay, this is ugly through-and-through. This is an absolute mess. The children are with you. Do you want them to be afraid everywhere they go? No, you want to be thinking on their behalf. If you feel there is a potential risk, think of how you can stay with them. "Yes, dear, I know you can go to the bathroom by yourself but I'm just going to go and make sure everything is okay, I'll be right outside the door."

Don't be separated by three rooms from your child. Be with your child. And of course, for anybody with multiple kids, that's always a challenge because one needs to do one thing, while the other needs to do something else. To the best of your ability stay with them.

Now, you don't want to alert them, you don't want to make them frightened, you don't want to have them react. Again, distance is your friend. If something starts to happen, stay with them, get out and go. That should be your priority above all.

If you're not with them, like I said, you have a whole new calculus to figure out or to set up. And there's no one-size-fits-all solution.

But now let's take the children into the school setting. Now the teacher has been given a set of rules to follow that are different from the rules I'm giving you. Generally, the teacher's first rule is to be accountable for all the kids, so all the kids have to stay in a group. If all the kids have to stay in a group, the only tactic available to them is to hide.

Now, the Sandy Hook massacre got re-processed into something I consider mass stupidity. All over the country, schools have erected six-foot-high fences to keep the bad guy out. Anybody who wants to kill a lot of people is going to have no trouble scaling a six-foot high fence—or even driving through it—and not a single kindergartener can scale it to get away from them.

We have established kill zones. I hate to say it that way, but we have done it. In the interest of safeguarding our children, we have put them at higher risk. So now you finish this book, and you decide you want to teach your children how to survive, and your children are being taught in a method opposite that of the school. Maybe you feel they know better. Maybe you feel they know how to survive. What have you done to your child when your child is the one running for the fence, is the *only one* running for the fence, and the teacher is screaming, "Bobby, Bobby, Bobby, come back!" with the door open with all the other kids and the shooter is looking for the first thing to draw his attention…

Q. *The first thing to draw his attention is your child.*

A. The first thing is your child.

Or it's the teacher with all the other kids. If all the rules, all the methods I just taught you were passed to your child and your child decides these are more important than the school's decisions to conceal the existence of the children, to hide in place, your child is in worse shape than if they hide in place.

Now, many schools have common corridors. They hide in a place with a single exit. A person comes in and kicks in a door, one after another until they're done, it's a repeat of Virginia Tech. This is going to contradict something I said earlier, but I would hope the teachers are being taught to get those kids out the window. That means they're coming above window level, which I said not to do, and that means there had better not be another shooter.

But if you do get the kids out, the next obstacle is to get around that fence that's "protecting" you, but you're trapped inside. Now, outside doors in a school are generally steel, they're pretty sturdy, they'll hold up well. Go back to Sandy Hook. Walk into the office, public and open, go into open hallways, it's over. The student and child situation is a mess right now. The guy came to shoot them knowing they'd be in their classrooms and the method we're talking about is that we are forcing them to stay there, turning off the lights, and hoping for the best. It is not a good situation. But it is the reality we're left with.

Like I said, if you teach your child that "don't hide, you need to put distance between yourself and the shooter" is the key to survival, then your panicked little child will be running up and down a six-foot high fence trying to figure out how in the world to escape that hell and have no hope at all. Everything I just taught you to survive will take the life of that child.

So the reality of it is: This needs to be a program for adults. This needs to be known by adults and the consciousness of the school systems needs to be raised. I regret having to say it, but I'm afraid a few more deaths will come between now and then, before our school safety experts wake up and realize they reacted wrong.

But once again, what is the national dialogue? We look for the weapons, not the attacker. So if you're the crazy bastard with a rap sheet a mile long who's carrying 14 guns, we're looking to see if we can spot guns, we don't care how nutty you are. You know, that's problem number one.

Now he's in. Oh, guns aren't allowed in the school so we'll stay put and we'll tell him to leave.

It doesn't take much brain power to figure out that that approach is not functional. He's there to kill.

Because we can't talk about the weapons, because we can't talk about mental illness, because we can't talk about utter rage, because we can't talk about the odd person, because we've killed that dialogue in our nation, he now has a free pass. And by building a six-foot high fence that he could scale blindfolded in the rain with no trouble, we have condemned our children. Because we're keeping him out, or so we wish to believe.

Once again, what did we do? We focused on the weapon! We ignored the person. There are gun museums with hundreds of firearms that have never attacked a human being. Day in and day out people come and look at them, and the guns don't attack any of those people.

It's the person that causes the problem. But we look at the weapon. So you know what? When we figure out that this does not work—fences and designated gun-free zones—what do we do next? We will add a metal detector.

Now we know that he's got the weapon, we still don't care about who or what he is. We don't care how nuts he is, who he is. We don't vet him for entry, but now we know he's armed. The detector goes beep. We react. He shoots. We lose.

Well, at least we knew about the device *[said with sarcasm]*. Yes, our current approaches are that ill-conceived. Pay no attention to that angry man in the doorway wearing the overcoat in 100-degree heat. Now, if you see that he has a weapon, then that's bad and we should do something! Why isn't the odd individual our clarion call? Why do we wait until we know that we are overmatched by an angry and armed assailant before we begin to do anything? We lose before the incident starts.

Now, what happened at the Pulse? There was a police officer at the door. Mateen wasn't allowed in with his guns, but one gunshot took care of that. Knowing they have the weapon doesn't stop the weapon. The weapon is not the issue, it's the person. And for all you know, the person broke in three weeks ago and left his stash of guns and bombs in a broom closet.

Q. If they are determined to get their weapons in, they'll find a way to do it.

A. Correct. So for the children, it is a mess. I hate to say that, but this needs to be an adult issue. And the education, as it gets promoted, as people start to realize we've already learned these lessons, may start to wake us up and change the way we operate. We've already learned that we're doing it wrong. Once that realization hits, hopefully the schools will rethink their approach to security. It's about the people coming in, it's about who and what they are. It's not about whether or not they're carrying something.

CHAPTER SIXTEEN

Final Thoughts

Question: *Is there anything we haven't discussed that you think is important to share?*

Answer: There are two key points to summarize. What do you do, and what do we need to do collectively?

The answer to what you do is simple and we've covered it: Do *what's important now*. WIN! We've talked about some techniques, but knowing when and how to apply them is the key.

What do we do collectively? Let's look at the situation holistically and see what is happening. Mass killings are on the increase. Our media reacts to social media's emotion and propels it forward, with our politicians throwing fuel on the fire. Before we know it, we have cities burning down for things that were not even real. The Baltimore Freddy Gray event led to mass destruction over a racial incident that did not exist. The Sanford Trayvon Martin incident inflamed and damaged a city before the facts came out, as we found that there was no racial epithet uttered by Zimmerman, there was no attack by Zimmerman, and the gun never left his pocket until it was found by Martin during a struggle. We reacted to emotion, not to fact. We spin up and burn our cities without justification and move along, ready to do it all over again. We remain angry, and our anger is fueled by rhetoric designed to make us buy more papers, watch more TV programs or listen to the agenda of our politicians ready to cure the very situation that never even occurred. A TED talk by Theo E.J. Wilson ("Theo E.J. Wilson: A black man goes undercover in the alt-right") made the brilliant point that social media today not only focuses advertising on our personal biases, but it also focuses our news media content on them. If we believe that one side or another of some political debate is correct, then today's technology ensures that we see the stories that support our beliefs—and not the ones that contradict them. Our own technology is helping us drive a wedge between each other.

For those on the edge, they find justification to kill. In a society so ready to burn, crash, steal and shoot over unsubstantiated emotion, are we not truly endorsing this behavior by our own? Where has the sense of right and wrong gone? The Golden Rule has been replaced by rage and destruction, and our society is paying the price.

In the end, the media and politicians seek that we focus on the devices, and ignore the actors, but it is the actors who are using the devices. The bomb must be built and triggered. The gun must be loaded and fired. The pressure cooker must be positioned and set to explode.

We can never successfully ban every possible means of killing—the device will always exist. Boston saw two pressure cookers with nails kill and maim many. 9/11 saw what Susan Olsen described as box cutters and knives kill thousands. Tylenol tampering killed with bottles of over the counter medicines in 1982. Sarin gas in a subway was a killer not long ago. Our shoes and our tiny bottles of liquids are now checked before each flight, as they are now weapons believed capable of bringing down aircraft. Needles, razors and other toxins have been placed in Halloween candy and fruits. Even piranha fish have been used to murder people.

Somehow, we need to realize that the device is only a means to an end that will be reached at the desire and intention of a person with malicious intent. We need to recognize the individual and stop encouraging him if we want the trend to reverse. Chasing devices leaves us all at high risk, recognizes the problem too late and guarantees loss of life. Meanwhile, the actors are becoming inflamed by our media, our politics, and our social media-fueled emotions. We inflame and empower them as we disarm and disempower our citizens who would otherwise oppose them. It makes no sense.

Passing another law appears proactive, but it is a simple measure that our politicians can perform to give us the illusion of progress. Well over half of the crimes in this nation are committed by drug gangs, and we have passed law after law making the drugs, the gangs, the guns, the violence and even the support of these things crimes. Just as making drugs illegal did nothing to stem the tide of the drug trade, making devices or circumstances illegal will have equal impotence against those wishing to kill their fellow man.

One international border station in El Paso, Texas is cited as having an average of *$7 million* per day in drug traffic crossing our border—just one spot! Yet we pass law after law about illegal immigration, border control, gun control, drug control with this strange belief that this time things will change. Things have changed, but not for the better. Yet whenever we find an issue, there is a media outlet ready to inflame it and generate fear, and a politician ready to sponsor yet another ill-conceived law to make us believe the situation is controllable. Yet no matter what "banned" thing you look at—drugs, prostitution, guns, crime, assaults, cyber theft, identity theft—the laws and bans have little impact. We've seen this for well over a century and somehow seem unable to figure out the math. Illegal behavior plus new laws equals continued illegal behavior. Legal behavior plus new laws equals reduced freedom, less safety and possible imprisonment of people doing the right things. How is that prohibition on alcohol working out again?

Our culture is the issue, not our laws. We need to remember the Golden Rule. We need to restore our recognition of our unity. We need to love our neighbor for being human, and not hate him for being anti-this or pro-that. We need to stop ignoring our fellow man who is in trouble or enraged, and instead be willing to stand up and offer him an ear or a hand. Once we remember that we are *all* equals, partners, brothers, sisters, and family in this human race, and once we start to care for and no longer ignore those in crisis, we will begin to see the violence—and the drugs, and the crime and even the use of devices—diminish. Our future salvation does not lie in immediate reaction—it lies in radical caring, in being willing to stand up and help *build* one another, no longer tearing each other down.

This is not a new idea. Many books, including many deemed holy by many faiths, have taught this lesson. It's time we figure out how to make these values real again, and how to put away the illogic and emotion fueled by our immediate sources of media, social media, and political agendas.

Love each other. The solution is truly that simple.

About the Expert

The Conversations series was designed to provide valuable information from expert sources on a variety of topics. Typically those experts use the books to promote themselves and their products or services. The expert for this book, How to Survive an Active Shooter, has declined to be identified. Most readers understand the explanation we provided in the introduction, but a few wanted to know more. When I posed the issue to the expert for this book, here is how he responded:

For both professional and personal reasons, I cannot reveal who I am. But even if you did know my name, odds are that you would not know me. You could look me up on the internet and find my name attached to many related presentations and reports, but I would just be another name to you.

There is no singular expert in this field, nor does anyone I know seek to be such a thing. If I asked you to name the leading expert in active shooter training, would you even imagine a name for someone?

Each "expert" simply had life experiences that taught him or her more than the typical citizen. That is my credential. I don't claim to be more or less knowledgeable than any other expert—just experienced enough to inform the general public.

I have worked with firearms of numerous calibers, some with bullets weighing more than 100 pounds. I have fired and disarmed explosives, bombs, and even missiles. I have worked closely with both the military and law enforcement. I have studied the physics of ballistics, explosions, lethalities, vulnerabilities, and countermeasures. I have studied and tested munitions, armor, and their interactions. Much of what I have done can only be done in specifically sanctioned areas under the most controlled of conditions and is not likely ever experienced by the general public.

I have also survived more than one terrorist attack of national significance, which led me to take the next logical steps in understanding this phenomenon of mass killings. I've interviewed experts, visited various test sites and training facilities, learned tactics, and seen many demonstrations of weaponry and its effects.

This explanation is my way of sharing with you, a member of society that I care about, a small piece of the lessons that I have learned from experience and research.

It's my hope that we cease to define each other by our partisan views, religions, and cultural differences and start to see each other as members of society that we care about. That's where the end of the violence will begin. However, so long as we seek to hate, to criticize, to fear, and to doubt, this scourge will continue to threaten us all.

I do not receive any monetary rewards from this endeavor. This book is completely a work of caring. I'm trying to set an example for us all to follow.

If we can care enough about each other to act with love and without malice, then maybe we can start to live a more peaceful existence. If your cultural teachings of doubt and distrust motivate you to believe that I have nothing to offer, then feel free to ignore what I've shared. I've done what I can to make the sense of it all clear to you.

No matter your personal trust issues with an anonymous source, please do take the time to grasp the message and content of this work. It's the work of a stranger trying to save your life.

If you found *How to Survive an Active Shooter: What You do Before, During and After an Attack Could Save Your Life* of value, please leave an honest review on Amazon and/or the online bookstore of your choice.

Reviews increase a book's ranking and visibility, and will increase the chance that more people will see this important information.

We also appreciate any mentions on your website or blog. Please send the URL to info@contacttcs.com so we can link back to it.

Appendix

How to Respond to an Active Shooter
Information from the U.S. Department of Homeland Security

Profile of an Active Shooter

An Active Shooter is an individual actively engaged in killing or attempting to kill people in a confined and populated area; in most cases, active shooters use firearms(s) and there is no pattern or method to their selection of victims. Active shooter situations are unpredictable and evolve quickly. Typically, the immediate deployment of law enforcement is required to stop the shooting and mitigate harm to victims. Because active shooter situations are often over within 10 to 15 minutes, before law enforcement arrives on the scene, individuals must be prepared both mentally and physically to deal with an active shooter situation.

Good practices for coping with an active shooter situation

• Be aware of your environment and any possible dangers.
• Take note of the two nearest exits in any facility you visit.
• If you are in an office, stay there and secure the door.
• If you are in a hallway, get into a room and secure the door.

• As a last resort, attempt to take the active shooter down. When the shooter is at close range and you cannot flee, your chance of survival is much greater if you try to incapacitate him/her.

Call 911 when it is safe to do so.

Vicinity

Quickly determine the most reasonable way to protect your own life. Remember that customers and clients are likely to follow the lead of employees and managers during an active shooter situation.

1. Evacuate. If there is an accessible escape path, attempt to evacuate the premises. Be sure to:
- Have an escape route and plan in mind
- Evacuate regardless of whether others agree to follow
- Leave your belongings behind
- Help others escape, if possible
- Prevent individuals from entering an area where the active shooter may be
- Keep your hands visible
- Follow the instructions of any police officers
- Do not attempt to move wounded people
- Call 911 when you are safe

2. Hide out. If evacuation is not possible, find a place to hide where the active shooter is less likely to find you. Your hiding place should:
- Be out of the active shooter's view
- Provide protection if shots are fired in your direction (i.e., an office with a closed and locked door)

• Not trap you or restrict your options for movement To prevent an active shooter from entering your hiding place, lock the door and blockade it with heavy furniture

If the active shooter is nearby:

- Lock the door
- Silence your cell phone and/or pager
- Turn off any source of noise (i.e., radios, televisions)
- Hide behind large items (i.e., cabinets, desks)
- Remain quiet if evacuation and hiding out are not possible:
- Remain calm
- Dial 911, if possible, to alert police to the active shooter's location
- If you cannot speak, leave the line open and allow the dispatcher to listen

3. Take action against the active shooter. As a last resort, and only when your life is in imminent danger, attempt to disrupt and/or incapacitate the active shooter by:

- Acting as aggressively as possible against him/her
- Throwing items and improvising weapons
- Yelling
- Committing to your actions

How to respond when law enforcement arrives

Law enforcement's purpose is to stop the active shooter as soon as possible. Officers will proceed directly to the area in which the last shots were heard.

- Officers usually arrive in teams of four (4)
- Officers may wear regular patrol uniforms or external bulletproof vests, Kevlar helmets, and other tactical equipment

- Officers may be armed with rifles, shotguns, handguns
- Officers may use pepper spray or tear gas to control the situation
- Officers may shout commands and may push individuals to the ground for their safety

How to react when law enforcement arrives:
- Remain calm, and follow officers' instructions
- Put down any items in your hands (i.e., bags, jackets)
- Immediately raise hands and spread fingers
- Keep hands visible at all times
- Avoid making quick movements toward officers such as holding on to them for safety
- Avoid pointing, screaming and/or yelling
- Do not stop to ask officers for help or direction when evacuating, just proceed in the direction from which officers are entering the premises

Information to provide to law enforcement or 911 operator:
- Location of the active shooter
- Number of shooters, if more than one
- Physical description of shooter(s)
- Number and type of weapons held by the shooter(s)
- Number of potential victims at the location

The first officers to arrive at the scene will not stop to help injured persons. Expect rescue teams comprised of additional officers and emergency medical personnel to follow the initial officers. These rescue teams will treat and remove any injured persons. They may also call upon able-bodied individuals to assist in removing the wounded from the premises. Once you have reached a safe location or an assembly point, you will likely be held in that area by law enforcement until the situation is under control, and all witnesses have been identified and questioned. Do not leave until law enforcement authorities have instructed you to do so.

Training your staff for an active shooter situation

To best prepare your staff for an active shooter situation, create an Emergency Action Plan (EAP) and conduct training exercises. Together, the EAP and training exercises will prepare your staff to effectively respond and help minimize loss of life.

Components of an Emergency Action Plan (EAP)

Create the EAP with input from several stakeholders including your human resources department, your training department (if one exists), facility owners / operators, your property manager, and local law enforcement and/or emergency responders. An effective EAP includes:

- A preferred method for reporting fires and other emergencies
- An evacuation policy and procedure
- Emergency escape procedures and route assignments (i.e., floor plans, safe areas)
- Contact information for, and responsibilities of individuals to be contacted under the EAP
- Information concerning local area hospitals (i.e., name, telephone number, and distance from your location)
- An emergency notification system to alert various parties of an emergency including:
  - Individuals at remote locations within premises
  - Local law enforcement
  - Local area hospitals

Components of Training Exercises

The most effective way to train your staff to respond to an active shooter situation is to conduct mock active shooter training exercises. Local law enforcement is an excellent resource for designing training exercises.

- Recognizing the sound of gunshots
- Reacting quickly when gunshots are heard and/or when a shooting is witnessed:
  - Evacuating the area
  - Hiding out
  - Acting against the shooter as a last resort
- Calling 911
- Reacting when law enforcement arrives
- Adopting the survival mindset during times of crisis

Additional Ways to Prepare For and Prevent an Active Shooter Situation

- **Preparedness**
  - Ensure that your facility has at least two evacuation routes
  - Post evacuation routes in conspicuous locations throughout your facility
  - Include local law enforcement and first responders during training exercises
  - Encourage law enforcement, emergency responders, SWAT teams, K-9 teams, and bomb squads to train for an active shooter scenario at your location
- **Prevention**
  - Foster a respectful workplace
  - Be aware of indications of workplace violence and take remedial actions accordingly

For more information on creating an EAP contact the U.S. Department of Labor, Occupational Health and Safety Administration, www.osha.gov.

Preparing for and managing an active shooter situation

Your human resources department and facility managers should engage in planning for emergency situations, including an active shooter scenario. Planning for emergency situations will help to mitigate the likelihood of an incident by establishing the mechanisms described below.

Human Resources' Responsibilities
- Conduct effective employee screening and background checks
- Create a system for reporting signs of potentially violent behavior
- Make counseling services available to employees
- Develop an EAP which includes policies and procedures for dealing with an active shooter situation, as well as after action planning

Facility Manager Responsibilities
- Institute access controls (i.e., keys, security system passcodes)
- Distribute critical items to appropriate managers/employees, including floor plans, keys and facility personnel lists and telephone numbers
- Coordinate with the facility's security department to ensure the physical security of the location
- Assemble crisis kits containing:
  - radios

- floor plans
- staff roster, and staff emergency contact numbers
- first aid kits
- flashlights

• Place removable floor plans near entrances and exits for emergency responders

• Activate the emergency notification system when an emergency situation occurs

Reactions of Managers During an Active Shooter Situation

Employees and customers are likely to follow the lead of managers during an emergency situation. During an emergency, managers should be familiar with their EAP, and be prepared to:

• Take immediate action

• Remain calm

• Lock and barricade doors

• Evacuate staff and customers via a preplanned evacuation route to a safe area

Assisting Individuals with Special Needs and/or Disabilities

• Ensure that EAPs, evacuation instructions and any other relevant information address to individuals with special needs and/or disabilities

• Your building should be handicap-accessible, in compliance with ADA requirements.

Recognizing potential workplace violence

An active shooter in your workplace may be a current or former employee, or an acquaintance of a current or former employee. Intuitive managers and coworkers may notice characteristics of potentially violent behavior in an employee. Alert your Human Resources Department if you believe an employee or coworker exhibits potentially violent behavior.

Managing the consequences of an active shooter situation

After the active shooter has been incapacitated and is no longer a threat, human resources and/or management should engage in post-event assessments and activities, including:

• An accounting of all individuals at a designated assembly point to determine who, if anyone, is missing and potentially injured

• Determining a method for notifying families of individuals affected by the active shooter, including notification of any casualties

• Assessing the psychological state of individuals at the scene, and referring them to health care specialists accordingly

• Identifying and filling any critical personnel or operational gaps left in the organization as a result of the active shooter

Lessons learned

To facilitate effective planning for future emergencies, it is important to analyze the recent active shooter situation and create an after action report. The analysis and reporting contained in this report are useful for:

• Serving as documentation for response activities

• Identifying successes and failures that occurred during the event

- Providing an analysis of the effectiveness of the existing EAP
- Describing and defining a plan for making improvements to the EAP

ABOUT JACQUELYN LYNN

Jacquelyn Lynn is a former business writer whose credits included more than 30 books when she followed God's call to become an inspirational author. Her other works include *Finding Joy in the Morning: You can make it through the night* and *Words to Work By: 31 devotions for the workplace based on the Book of Proverbs* as well as the meditations in *Christian Meditations* and *Faith Words,* two Christian adult coloring books.

For more information or to contact her:

CreateTeachInspire.com

Conversations is a series of affordably-priced books based on in-depth conversations with leading subject matter experts.

Titles in the **Conversations** series include:

Is Your Website Legal? How To Be Sure Your Website Won't Get You Sued, Shut Down or in Other Trouble

The Power of Mobile Apps: How a Mobile App Can Increase Sales, Strengthen Customer Loyalty and Grow Your Bottom Line—No Matter What Business You're In

Put Your Website to Work: How Lawyers, Therapists, Coaches and Other Professional Service Providers Can Turn Their Websites Into Money-making Machines

Get Your Book Published: How to Choose Between Self-publishing, Traditional Publishing or Pay-to-publish Options

The Time Is Right for Direct Mail: How Any Business or Nonprofit Can Use Direct Mail to Increase Revenue & Strengthen Customer/Donor Relationships

The Value of Creativity: How Developing Your Personal Creativity Can Have an Amazingly Positive Impact on Your Happiness, Health, Business Success and Life in General

To see a complete list of titles and expert sources with links to order, visit createteachinspire.com/conversations.

To suggest a topic for a Conversations book, send us a message at CreateTeachInspire.com/contact.

Adult Coloring Books

More and more adults are coloring to reduce stress and enhance their own creativity.

If you are a coloring enthusiast, you'll want to check out the adult coloring books from Tuscawilla Creative Services.

Finding Joy in the Morning
A collection of 60 beautiful images and meditations designed to help you find the joy God intends for you every day.

Faith Words: Color the words that inspire you every day
An adult coloring book for people of faith. Color the words and meditations that will motivate and inspire you every day.

Christian Meditations
Color your faith with this collection of 60 beautiful images.

The Sebring Experience
Color these pictures of cars, people, and action from the legendary 12 Hours of Sebring.

The pictures are illustrations created from Jerry D. Clement's photographs or designed by Jerry specifically for these coloring books. Meditations are by inspirational author Jacquelyn Lynn.

Available on Amazon

Finding Joy in the Morning
You can make it through the night

How to enjoy incredible peace during some of life's toughest times!

This is not a self-help book, this is an I-can't-do-it-alone book.

This updated and expanded edition of *Finding Joy in the Morning* shows you how to surrender the natural human proclivity to try to be in control so that you'll know the peace and find the joy that comes with knowing God is always with you and always in control.

The completely new Part II gives you more than 40 things you can do on a daily basis to bring joy to your life and be a catalyst for creating joy for others.

Let these simple but powerful strategies bring you joy every morning, even after life's darkest nights.

Available on Amazon and at your favorite bookstore

For more information about books by Jacquelyn Lynn, visit **CreateTeachInspire.com**.

Words to Work By

31 devotions for the workplace based on the Book of Proverbs

Messages of inspiration and motivation based on the teachings of the world's greatest business advisor: King Solomon.

Our faith is a part of who we are, and we don't leave it at the door when we go to work. But sometimes in the mad chaos of today's business world, we need the peace, comfort, and guidance that a brief devotion and prayer can bring.

Words to Work By provides those devotions and prayers.

Available at your favorite online bookstore

www.ingramcontent.com/pod-product-compliance
Lightning Source LLC
Chambersburg PA
CBHW071708020426
42333CB00017B/2185